Journal
of a
Country Priest

Father Matt Pennington

Journal
of a
Country Priest

Kenos Press

An Imprint of Six Degrees Publishing Group

Portland · Oregon

Published in the USA by Kenos Press
An Imprint of Six Degrees Publishing Group

Kenos Press and the portrayal of the
outpouring of water from a vessel is
a trademark of Six Degrees Publishing Group, Inc.

ISBN: 978-1-942497-45-5 (Hardcover Edition)

Book Design by Denise C. Williams, Six Degrees Publishing Group
Copyediting by Rebecca Board Liljenstolpe (rblwriter.com)

Cover photos:
Father Matt Pennington: by Mary Ann Stater
Vineyard: Malcolm Carlaw (visualjaunts.com/travel-photography/
landscape-photography-malcolm-carlaw.html)
San Luis Obispo/Cerro San Luis Peak: Shutterstock
Bishop's Peak 2009: Erron Evans

Printed in the United States of America

FIRST EDITION
February 13, 2019

1 3 5 7 9 10 8 6 4 2

For all those who believe in the

infinite possibilities of God ~

Prologue

THERE IS A SMALL TOWN off the central coast of California. Homes, businesses and a university are nestled between mountains. When you drive about you see cattle, vineyards, horses and orchards. After twenty-five years of priesthood, I chose this country place to continue my story with God. The God who speaks in a tiny whispering sound and the God who opens a passageway through the sea. This journal contains my dreams and visions as I make my way in an enchanted countryside.

My *Journal of a Country Priest* is not constructed as a story from beginning to end; rather each day, each question, each quote is its own entity. Read the journal one day at a time and know that the considerations and ruminations continue in my life and in yours. I share these days with you for I feel that we are all asking the same questions about life, about love and about God.

Father Matt Pennington ~

DAY 1

Shangri-La

April 8, 2013

THERE HAVE BEEN two movies made from James Hilton's novel *Lost Horizon*. The moment I love in both movies involves the *cave*.

In the movie version of the story, a group of Americans are fleeing a country under siege and find themselves hijacked on a small plane heading into the Himalayan Mountains. The plane crashes and the pilot is killed. The passengers with almost no provisions await their death in the hull of the aircraft. A few days in, they are discovered by members of a community that exists in a mountain valley called Shangri-La. The snow is raging, the wind is devastating and the journey to the valley is arduous and dangerous. The people from the plane are exhausted from the climb and close to surrender when they enter a cave. As they enter the opening, the snow is blowing furiously and as they make their way in, they see that it is not a cave but a passageway that opens into a fantastic, verdant valley full of sunshine. They look back at the entrance and see a storm, and ahead light and peace. Shangri-La is a utopia where stress and conflict do not exist. There is no illness in Shangri-La, and the people who live there strive for harmony and understanding.

I am a Catholic priest celebrating twenty-five years of ministry. It has been a difficult period of time to be a priest: conflicting views on orthodoxy, politics and spirituality, pedophilia and unimaginable shame. Alongside all that, I have found myself required to step into a variety of complex administrative circumstances with remarkably little experience or expertise. Looking back, it all seems a bit tumultuous—like the plane crashing in the Himalayans. However, through a remarkable chain of events, I find myself today in a small, green valley near the sea on the coast of California. It is unlike any place I have ever lived. I sail through town virtually traffic free. The residents greet one another in a peaceful and friendly fashion. And the church to which I have been assigned is small, intimate and welcoming.

I feel a bit like the survivors of the plane crash in *Lost Horizon* coming to an enchanted place after a long and difficult journey. It is here in these pages I hope to capture the story of my life and work in a unique setting where I believe God has brought me. All my life I have read stories and watched movies about people going to a strange and wondrous place where amazing things happen.

Here I am and the story is about to begin . . .

Day 2

Sound

April 9, 2013

Then the Lord said to Elijah:
Go outside and stand on the mountain before
the Lord;
the Lord will be passing by.
A strong and heavy wind was rending the
mountains and crushing rocks before the Lord—
but the Lord was not in the wind.
After the wind there was an earthquake—but the
Lord was not in the earthquake.
After the earthquake there was a fire—
but the Lord was not in the fire.
After the fire there was a tiny whispering sound.
     −1 Kings 19:11-12

I T'S QUIET HERE.

I feel my life transitioning into a stage of quiet. I am actually not one of those clerics always bemoaning the lack of silence and contemplation in society. I enjoy noisy, electric places. I spent a week in New York City this year and was thrilled every morning when my feet hit the pavement: traffic, crowds, theatres, restaurants, museums all swirling around me in a mad rush of sound and light. It's wonderful and exhausting.

However, here in this small town I feel the seduction of quiet and peace. In my former parish I practically lived underneath Highway 1. I never slept with windows open or enjoyed a sense of stillness. Here I keep the doors and windows wide so that the music of nature floods the rooms. I am interested in the different times of day supporting unique sounds from nature. Early mornings and twilights are my favorite moments.

One evening the sky was turning this ripe plum color when a silver-grey fog rolled over the mountains near the church and it was as if the entire neighborhood had been hushed. I am certain I heard the fog make a sound like the comforter on my bed when I pull it over freshly laundered sheets.

When I am in the church celebrating daily mass, I never hear the sound of a car horn. On those mornings the church feels nestled in some alternative universe. Although the Mass is full of words and movements, I need only sit still in my chair for the assembly to relax into a rich, luxurious silence. Quiet in church is like being wrapped in some fantastically expensive fabric that surrounds the individual in comfort and clarity. Words, music and speech are all necessary tools that bring a disparate group into public prayer, but it is in quiet that I can finally stop fretting, planning, dictating and orchestrating. It is in the silence of this place I might be able to actually speak to God and perhaps more importantly listen . . . to the tiny whispering sound.

Day 3

Treading

April 12, 2013

THERE IS A LITTLE GIRL in my parish who dreams of being an Olympic swimmer. While listening to her story, I was reminded of the games in London last summer. Watching on television was a glimpse into another world: the world of athletes trained, analyzed and groomed into perfect specimens. I sometimes felt as if I were watching characters from a science fiction film. When you hear the broadcasters describe their backstory, it is almost a relief to hear that some of them have taken time off to recover and regroup after years of grueling training and competition. When you look into their faces and their almost desperate glimpses at the scoreboards after competition, I read sadness not joy. Even in triumph I observe relief that all of this might finally be over.

Among the events I witnessed on television was the water

polo. I marveled at the athletes' ability to tread water for such long periods of time. And not only treading water but also simultaneously strategizing, balancing, surprising and striving. And even when the ball is not in play, they need to tread water to keep afloat. It is a metaphor for certain expressions of life today.

I often feel that families are treading water. The expectations for family life appear Herculean. There are those rare family exceptions who choose to step away from extraneous activities of modern family life and choose instead to embrace a simpler and more manageable lifestyle. It takes a certain courage to take such a step: the courage to be different, to not necessarily participate, to not "keep up" or do what others expect you should. Such a person is unafraid to grab onto the side of the pool and rest awhile as all the others are treading, treading, treading.

Day 4

Connection

April 17, 2013

PARISHIONERS ARE ALWAYS giving me material for my preaching. They will see a movie or read a magazine article and immediately pass the link, novel, TV listing or DVD into my hands with great enthusiasm and the urgently voiced statement, "This would make a great homily!" Rarely does the aforementioned content inspire me and, frankly, only occasionally do I find the time to read or watch the material in question. Imagine my surprise when I actually viewed a compelling parishioner-recommended TED Talk on my computer given by researcher Brene Brown. She has been involved for many years researching vulnerability, courage, authenticity and shame and how those various states of mind affect our lives.

Brown found after years of compiling data that being

connected to one another is our ultimate purpose in life and that shame prevents that connectivity from happening. She defines our need to be a people living "wholeheartedly," which means cultivating the courage necessary to be vulnerable. She states that vulnerability is the birthplace of joy, creativity, belonging, love and everything else of real value in life.

What a terrifying idea. Imagine after years of cultivating independence, wealth, credentials, vocabulary and the façade of self-esteem—imagine finding that the truly essential quality required for fulfillment is to make oneself vulnerable. And yet, that concept lines up with the Jesus story.

Jesus is always the vulnerable one. He is the one to reach out, to sacrifice, to empower, to trust and to believe that, even in fear and bewilderment, we are connected to this wondrous God. How continually strange to observe that the thing we most fear is the very thing that saves us.

Day 5

Boston

April 19, 2013

TWO YEARS AGO, I was on a non-stop flight from Manhattan to the West Coast. About forty minutes into the flight the plane began to experience extreme turbulence. For almost an hour the plane was in a severe state of twisting, vibrating and dropping. Already a nervous flyer (*and wound a bit tighter than the average person under the best of circumstances*) I found myself in a state of near panic. Nothing could distract me—not a book; not the iPad; not the chant track on my iPod. I finally sat up straight in the seat, planted both feet on the floor and began to pray and breathe deeply. My prayer was not elaborate or complex—just the Lord's Prayer, the Hail Mary and the Glory Be to God, calmly between breaths. I cannot write that I returned to normal (*whatever THAT is*), but I did feel less unglued. The praying made me feel accompanied. And it occurs to me the most frightening thing of all is believing we are alone.

I have spent a seemingly extraordinary amount of my life in fear. I was afraid of that baseball hurtling toward my face in Little League. I have been paralyzed by the possibility of failure, rejection, criticism, loneliness and the future. I was afraid to get on an airplane after September 11 and frightened of the flu shot in 2012. I get worried when I cannot remember someone's name or the details of a novel I read last month. Currently I worry about the safety of children in schools, and now apparently standing on the sidelines at a marathon in Boston, Massachusetts is akin to being in a combat zone.

Thomas L. Friedman in his *New York Times* editorial on April 16 decodes the terrorist's intention of creating fear in the everyday: [1]

> *That is the signature of modern terrorism: to turn*
> *routine items from our lives into bombs: the shoe,*
> *the backpack, the car, the airplane, the cellphone,*
> *the laptop, the garage door opener, fertilizer, the*
> *printer, the pressure cooker—so that everything*
> *and everyone becomes a source of suspicion.*

He goes on to observe that we cannot allow ourselves to be hoodwinked into believing that we are alone and without resources—for we have one another and we have great faith. He writes:

> *Watch the video of the bombing aftermath, notice*
> *how many people you see running toward the*
> *blast within seconds to help, even though more*
> *bombs easily could have been set to explode there.*

I am so very weary of being afraid and aware that Christ is always encouraging the human person to be fearless. Observing the courage of the people in Boston and the fortitude and generosity of the parishioners in every parish I have ever been assigned helps to alleviate the fear and paralysis. Because after all, planes crash, cancer cells multiply, bombs will detonate but somehow it makes me feel a little bit calmer to know that when that moment comes and I am no longer who I was, someone will come running toward me so I will not be alone.

> *Let nothing disturb you,*
> *let nothing frighten you.*
> *All things are passing.*
> *God never changes.*
> *Patient endurance*
> *attains all things God possesses.*
> *In nothing is wanting,*
> *alone God suffices.*
> —Saint Teresa of Avila

DAY 6

Angels

April 23, 2013

> *See, I am sending an angel before you,*
> *to guard you on the way*
> *and bring you to the place I have prepared.*
> *Be attentive to him and heed his voice.*
>> *–Exodus 23:20-21*

IN 1991, THE FILMMAKER Lawrence Kasdan released a movie entitled *Grand Canyon*. The film is about alienation and connection between various characters who live in the Los Angeles area. In one scene the actor, Kevin Klein, is waiting to traverse a busy downtown intersection on foot and, being distracted, he attempts to cross the dangerous street before it is safe. As he steps off the curb, someone from behind grabs his jacket and pulls him back, just as an enormous city bus whooshes across and would have killed him. He is dazed and as the light changes and the crowd begins to swarm past him to the other side, he realizes he has no idea who saved him, so he shouts out "*thank you.*" And a young woman dressed in work clothes and a baseball cap turns and with a smile and a wave says, "*A pleasure,*" before disappearing into the throng.

There is something about that scene that delights me—the idea that there are angels among us who protect us as we face the dangers of the world.

I am reminded of the real world angels who come to the rescue every day in catastrophes. The people who ran into the blast zone in Boston last week to assist the wounded, the community in east Texas who opened their houses to families newly homeless after the explosion of the fertilizer plant. The courage and hope demonstrated by adults who adopt small children already addicted to cocaine, and the countless numbers of individuals who volunteer in soup kitchens, nursing and maternity homes and prisons.

I believe God will send angels to us when we find ourselves shattered and frightened. And I pray that we will *be* those angels of mercy to those in need when the unimaginable happens and our world is exploding around us.

DAY 7

Presence

April 26, 2013

Behold, God's dwelling is with the human race.
He will dwell with them and they will be
his people
and God himself will always be with them as
their God.
He will wipe every tear from their eyes,
and there shall be no more death or mourning,
wailing or pain, for the old order has
passed away.
  –Revelation 21:1-4

THE EXCERPT PRESENTED ABOVE is taken from the book of Revelation which is a collection of visions had by John the seer.

This particular passage in the slate of this Sunday's readings presents a Utopian environment where the human family is restored to that perfect relationship with God. A place where there is no longer any pain, suffering or confusion.

This vision reminds me of all the moments I have sat with people *in this world* wracked with unimaginable anguish. In those moments when parishioners are encountering their worst possible life experience, they look to their parish priest to somehow put their story into some kind of perspective that brings them comfort and insight. In that regard I have been a miserable failure. Often I find myself silenced by the enormity of the other's grief and searching desperately for something . . . something to say that will remove some modicum of their sorrow.

How, I ask you, when someone is wailing in a hospital waiting room does one attempt to explain the complexity of the theology of suffering? Where are those magic sound bites that loop a comforting ribbon around the box of another's torment? Is it possible to find spiritual perspective in a culture where people shoot children in a school or place bombs on a busy street corner?

I am, as usual, without answers to any of these questions. However, my lived experience is that when someone is falling apart, they rarely have the expectation that you are going to put them together again. What would appear to be comforting is that you are there. That you return the phone call or walk into the Trauma Center. Often an onrushing of gratitude is extended when you simply listen, or hold someone's hand or offer to voice a prayer. Amazingly, just being there would seem to offer great consolation. I suppose you could say that about Jesus: he did not always prevent, or heal, or appease. Nevertheless he was present in affliction, in rejection, in hunger and in sorrow. So I must accept that I cannot remove the cross the other person is struggling with. For now, I shall continue to consecrate the Eucharist, positively interpret the Sacred Scriptures and look into the eyes of the person in front of me.

I am here. I am right here . . . that's all I have.

Day 8

Joy

April 30, 2013

A time to weep, and a time to laugh;
a time to mourn, and a time to dance.
—Ecclesiastes

MANY YEARS AGO, I met a friend for lunch in New York City before seeing a play. During the meal he took a call from his mother that upset him terribly. I could feel the afternoon's excitement slipping away and no amount of banter on my part seemed to affect his darkening mood. We dolefully took a cab to the theatre district and went to see the actor Martin Short in a musical revue he had created in celebration of his life. The play lasted approximately an hour and a half, and we never stopped laughing from the beginning to the end. We floated out of the theatre on a cloud of well-being. I've never forgotten how that show radically shifted the mood of the day and how laughter is a crucial element in the design of one's life.

For me good humor is like a hook on the end of a fishing line . . . it pulls me in. Sometimes just the sound of a stranger laughing in a public place can transition my disposition. I have actually had to pull my car over to the side of the road because my companion was making me laugh with such vigor, I was no longer sure I could navigate the vehicle safely.

If you can find friends and colleagues who make you laugh so hard you need to stop driving a car, I believe you have found the most precious jewel. Think about it—as we trudge through life, paying bills, completing tasks, worrying, saving, planning, reconstructing—don't we all need a tiny sip of wine, a little block of chocolate and a friend who reminds us of the divine comedy? Really . . . in the end, what else is there?

> *When the Lord brought back the captives*
> *of Zion,*
> *we were like men dreaming.*
> *Then our mouth was filled with laughter,*
> *and our tongue with rejoicing.*
> *Then they said among the nations,*
> *"The Lord has done great things for them."*
> *The lord has done great things for us;*
> *we are glad indeed.*
> —Psalm 126

DAY 9

Change

May 3, 2013

"Who are you?" said the Caterpillar.
This was not an encouraging opening
for a conversation.
Alice replied, rather shyly, "I—I hardly know, Sir,
just at present—at least I know who I was when
I got up this morning, but I think I must have
changed several times since then."
     –Alice's Adventures in Wonderland
     Lewis Carroll (1832–1898)

THE SEMINARY I ATTENDED has a custom of inviting priests to return to the institution and concelebrate a mass on the occasion of the twenty-fifth year of priesthood or what is known as the cleric's "silver jubilee." I never attend reunions of any kind and nearly declined this invitation. However, I had not seen any of my seminary classmates in a quarter of a century and suspected this would be my last chance to be with people who were with me at a defining moment in my life. In my wildly vivid imagination, I presumed they would all be altered, somehow more mature, worldly, opinionated and therefore insufferable (*don't ask me to explain—it would simply take too long*).

What I found is that all of us were almost exactly the same, only more defined. The characteristics that were with us in our early twenties were made sharper and more profound through time.

I suspect many of us focus attention on how our circumstances have changed us. We regret the hasty decisions and mishaps. We wish we could revisit the past and adjust the undesirable route directed by life's wonky GPS.

But what if regardless of the decisions and phases of our lives—we would be the same people we are right now? What if living and the adventure of our existence merely polish and highlight who we really are? If we believe that, is it possible to abandon regret? Could we be free from remorse and despondency if we could acknowledge that the soul of who we are will be revealed in success or in failure, in abundance or poverty, in wisdom or in foolishness? If we are made in the image and likeness of God, perhaps life's pleasures and disappointments have the potential of gradually exposing courage, perseverance and generosity. Who we really are can shine forth regardless of our life story. And who you really are is a child of God.

> *I saw the angel in the marble and carved until*
> *I set him free.*
> 　　　 –Michelangelo

Day 10

Perseverance

May 7, 2013

The one that endures to the end shall be saved.
–Matthew 10:22

HAD BREAKFAST WITH THE RETIRED PASTOR of my church. There was no real agenda except to catch up with one another's life. However, I was interested in steering the conversation into some areas of parish history so that I would have perspective about various issues. As I listened to this seventy-year-old priest I was conscious of how hard he has worked all his ministerial life. And not only how hard he worked but how much he cared. After twenty-five years of ministry, I often find myself worn by the increasing demands of Church life. When confronted with obstacles and negativity, my inner voice tells me to flee, abandon and run! *Mayday! Lower the lifeboats and PUSH OFF!!* So when I find myself in the company of people who persevere in the midst of disappointment, I am filled with great respect and humility.

There are circumstances where walking away is absolutely the prudent response, but when I see a couple celebrating a forty- or fifty-year anniversary and still enjoying each other's company or a long-term teacher with continued zeal for enlightening students, I am filled with admiration and wonder.

There are clerics who work hard to preach sermons and homilies so that congregations can be strengthened and nourished. I encounter weary employees standing behind cash registers never too bored to offer a smile and an encouraging greeting. We inhabit a culture where everything is becoming more litigious, more labyrinthine, more exhausting and consequently more and more of us walk away from churches, schools, businesses and relationships out of frustration and defeat. The people who endure with good humor and faith are my heroes. Because of these living saints, I think I can keep smiling, keep praying, keep searching for the next belly laugh and keep believing that with God anything is possible.

> *He that can't endure the bad will not live to see*
> *the good.*
> > —Jewish Proverb

Day 11

Father

May 10, 2013

> My son, take care of your father when he is old;
> grieve him not as long as he lives.
> Even if his mind fail, be considerate with him;
> revile him not in the fullness of your strength.
> For kindness to a father will
> not be forgotten;
> it will serve as a sin offering—
> it will take lasting root.
> In time of tribulation it will be
> recalled to your advantage,
> like warmth upon frost it will
> melt away your sins.
>
>   –Sirach 3:12–15

M Y FATHER DIED TODAY. His body had been crashing for some time. He was just released yesterday from the hospital and was placed in nursing care. He had his breakfast and went to sit in a chair and he slipped away. Such a quiet exit for such a big man.

By the standards of history he was an old man. When I watch home movies of him in his youth, he is like a God. Don Draper with the black shiny hair and the dark framed glasses of the 60s. He was lean, handsome and seemingly without insecurity. Some years ago, he lost his powerful voice and hearing. He did not see well and was often distressed by physical pain.

My mysterious child/parent relationship has been fraught with all the colors of the emotional pallet. However, of this I am sure: my father would have surrendered anything for me. There is no amount of money, no extra days of life, any dream or wish or temptation that would have caused him to waver in his desire for my happiness and well-being. I have no uncertainty regarding his love and pride in my accomplishments, and I wish that all children could experience the unreserved love of a parent. It is my most precious possession.

May the angels lead him into paradise;
and may perpetual light shine upon him.

Day 12

Unconditional

May 14, 2013

So he got up and went back to his father. While
he was still a long way off, his father caught sight
of him, and was filled with compassion. He ran to
his son, embraced him and kissed him. His son said
to him, 'Father, I have sinned against heaven and
against you: I no longer deserve to be called you son.'

But his father ordered his servants, 'Quickly bring
the finest robe and put it on him; put a ring on his
finger and sandals on his feet. Take the fatted calf
and slaughter it. Then let us celebrate with a feast,
because this son of mine was lost, and has been
found.' Then the celebration began.

–Luke 15:20

KEEP THINKING ABOUT UNCONDITIONAL LOVE. In the recent death of my father, I believe I have lost the one person who loved me unconditionally. Don't we all long to be loved without the usual boundaries? What a bewitching concept: to be forgiven, applauded and admired long after everyone else has grown bored or disenchanted. Furthermore, do we not wish to love our spouse/child/parent free from all the predictable limitations? And is our love for others not front- and back-loaded with expectations and requirements? What is "unconditional love?" And does it really exist?

Jesus appeared to love those around him without condition. He could be impatient with his companions and he was ready to scold those whose behavior was contemptuous, but he appeared willing to extend sincere love and perspective to everyone with whom he came in contact. In his parable, Jesus uses the Prodigal Father as an illustration of God's unconditional connection with human beings. In spite of being ignored and used, the Father is willing to forgive, embrace and renew relationships in spite of the ugliness of past decisions.

So how do we get to THAT place? That place where the love we have for our family and friends transcends pettiness, competition and disillusionment?

Vera Nazarian, in her book The Perpetual Calendar of Inspiration, writes that there are three requirements for unconditional love: Acceptance, Understanding and Appreciation.[1] Those are some heavy-duty words—beautiful to read and ponder when one is sipping tea and gazing into an imaginary fireplace—but rather cumbersome when one is attempting to refinance a long-term mortgage and navigate a gridlocked freeway! However, what if I were to write those magic words in the palm of my hand, on sticky notes placed upon the bathroom mirror, as screen savers for the computer?

If I were to consider the qualities of acceptance, understanding and appreciation throughout my day, I cannot help but wonder if there might gradually be an infiltration of these qualities *into* my everyday life? And if these characteristics began to manifest themselves more frequently in my thoughts and speech would I not find myself possessing more friendship, more support and a greater depth of love in my life? And while not unconditional, *(we may only get one or two of those in a lifetime)* anything that cultivates the lifelong goal of loving and being loved is a worthwhile effort . . . don't you agree?

DAY 13

Friends

May 17, 2013

> *Of all things that wisdom provides for living one's entire life in happiness, the greatest by far is the possession of friendship.*
>   –Epicurus

ONCE I HAD A FRIEND WHO LIVED in a small town and was exposed in a terrible scandal. She was miserable and found that many of her "friends" would actually cross the street to avoid her. In an effort to console, I told her that one advantage to her wretched situation is that now she knew who her real friends were. Her response: *"Who cares! I never really wanted to know that particular piece of information."*

I have always valued friendship and have been a person

who has contributed a significant amount of time and energy in cultivating and maintaining relationships. In spite of all that effort, I never truly understood the profound experience of friends in the midst of suffering.

My email, voicemail and the texts on my mobile phone were full of tender and thoughtful communications in the aftermath of my father's death. It was remarkable how consoling those messages were to my broken heart. Upon my return home from my father's funeral there was a stack of greeting cards, mass intentions and small gifts. Each contact carried with it a ping of direct loving energy.

While I am still attempting to decode the feelings and sensations of suddenly losing a loving parent, my immediate thought is how alone one feels—a major touchstone, a completely reliable source of unconditional love vanishes and one feels disoriented. So suddenly you're alone, shocked and frightened and then the voices of friends shower over you like music, like the smell of freshly baked bread coming out of the oven, like the voice of your physician telling you he was mistaken and you are going to be just fine.

"Well, so what," says my disheartened friend from the past. *"What am I supposed to do with all THAT?"* Well this: Pick up the phone and make the call. Go get the card and spend five minutes composing a sincere message; send the text; buy the present. Do it today, because you will never know the tremendous feeling of safety and perspective you will bring to someone you love. It changes everything . . .

Because you have the Lord for your refuge;
you have made the Most High your stronghold.
No evil shall befall you, nor shall affliction come
near your tent,
for to his angels he has given command about you,
that they guard you in all your ways.
Upon their hands they shall bear you up, lest you
dash your foot against a stone.

> –Psalm 91

DAY 14

Words

May 21, 2013

Things are not all so comprehensible and
expressible as one would mostly have us believe;
most events are inexpressible, taking place in
a realm which no word has ever entered, and
more inexpressible than all else are works of art,
mysterious existences, the life of which, while ours
passes away, endures.

> –Rainer Maria Rilke, *Letters to a*
> *Young Poet*, February 13, 1903

I NEVER GO TO WEDDING RECEPTIONS. It's too lonely. Most of those events are made up of couples and I feel isolated in those settings. Also, the guests are often uncomfortable when the priest sits with them. They retreat into grim silence as if afraid I am going to suggest they enter into a long overdue *Confession* before dessert. Or worse, they ask probing questions about my personal life that make me squirm. I just don't go. It's easier to decline.

However, last night I attended a rehearsal dinner of a wedding I am celebrating today. The meal was held at a converted cottage in a residential neighborhood. The little house was covered in ivy and jasmine and inside the small rooms had been opened up into extended expanses of gleaming wood floors and plastered walls. We were seated at a long farm house table groaning under the weight of flowers and flickering candles. There were wood-fired pizzas with cheese and asparagus and pressed greens. We had pâté and fresh breads for appetizers and then mixed green salads with rough cut hazelnuts in a vinaigrette. We could choose our entrée and I selected a perfectly cooked piece of salmon with a dot of cream sitting in quinoa. Everything was delicious and beautiful in a room filled with laughter and happy people. I was sitting one down from a young San Francisco woman who explained to me that she volunteers two days a week on an Alzheimer's hotline. People call with questions or *"sometimes they just need to talk."* Two full days a week this lady goes into a room and voluntarily listens to strangers who are living in a nightmare.

Two. Full. Days! That is what I call holiness. And sitting across from this living saint was her mother who volunteers in a Memory Care Unit of a local nursing home and brings drawing paper and watercolors, inviting the patients to paint for a couple of hours. She explained to me, *"The Alzheimer's patient is blocked—they cannot enable their brain to communicate in a traditional way, so the painting becomes a channel for expression."* In other words, the painting frees the patient to express themselves in a way words no longer can. This intrigues me. The idea that we use symbols as a way of approaching something intangible. Actually, we do this all the time:

When we pray, we use words (*which are limited forms of communication at best*) to express our longing, gratitude and need to the unimaginable wonder that is God. The rosary is a symbol that provides a tactile experience of entering into the presence of the Holy Mother. Swimming is an environment where we seek to be buoyant. Making love becomes a place of profound intimacy. Playing a musical instrument, sculpting with a blob of clay and hiking in nature all become channels of non-verbal communication. These places and experiences provide an atmosphere where words and logic no longer matter because we have transitioned into a mysterious place of transcendence. A place where the woodworking or the quilting or the watercolor *transcend* the blocked, wounded or insecure places in the mind/body and open us to something greater, something unknown, something beyond our ability to completely understand.

DAY 15

∝

Courage

May 24, 2013

> *Whoever puts his hand to the plow but keeps*
> *looking back is unfit for the reign of God.*
>   –Jesus

I HAVE BEEN WATCHING THE TELEVISION coverage of the Oklahoma disaster and was initially struck by the lack of self-pity evidenced by the residents who had lost their homes. Maybe it was the people the reporters chose to interview or the specific families the editors featured, but I noticed a consistent expression of gratitude and hope on behalf of individuals whose homes and memories had been swept away in an instant.

I suppose that when your entire world is squashed and you look around in a daze and find that the people you love most—

the one, completely irreplaceable substance in your life—intact, nothing else really matters.

I have spent a good amount of time in my life feeling sorry for myself and bemoaning the injustice of certain circumstances in my story. And in Oklahoma there is an entire community of people who have lost everything and yet they are full of courage, faith and a desire to rebuild. How wonderful to crawl out of an underground chamber, witness utter devastation and with a shrug of your shoulders decide to get to work. Where does that come from and more importantly . . . how do I get some of that elixir?

I am weary of listening to people complain about the petty injustices of their lives and more significantly, I am sick of hearing it come out of my own mouth! When I look at those teachers who threw themselves on top of their students to save them from a cyclone, when I listen to a ninety-year-old woman whose home has been destroyed twice by nature, when I witness a parent burying their child and offering comfort to the mourners, I wonder if it is possible to abandon past behavior and become such a noble, courageous and hopeful person overnight? Is it possible to begin a new day without complaint or self-pity or morbid obsession with the past?

George Elliot said, "It's never too late to become the person you might have been." I don't want to wait for an earthquake or a plague to demonstrate courage—I would prefer to climb out of the dark, subterranean shelter of the past and begin right now to be the person God created me to be. Would you like to join me?

Courage is not the absence of fear,
but rather the judgment that something else
is more important than fear.
    —Meg Cabot

Day 16

Perspective

May 28, 2013

JEANNETTE WALLS IS AN AUTHOR who wrote a best-selling book about being raised by horribly neglectful parents who were indifferent to the basic needs of their children. She is releasing a new book soon and was interviewed last week by *The New York Times Magazine* about her current life in the Virginia countryside where she provides a home and support for her mother in spite of a traumatic upbringing.[1] The NYT interviewer asked Walls, "How could you forgive your mother for the way you were raised?" Walls answered, "It's really not forgiveness in my opinion. It's acceptance. She's never going to be the sort of mother who wants to take care of me." I found myself considering that distinction: Is acceptance easier to embrace than forgiveness? Certainly *accepting* one's past and the people who are responsible for it is a very different point of view than *forgiving* the personalities and circumstances of one's journey.

Hmmm . . . acceptance vs. forgiveness . . . is one easier to embrace than the other? I began pondering this while peddling madly on the stationary bike at my gym and going absolutely nowhere. This is the moment when I should be offering sage advice on the nuance of one vs. the other. The cloudy skies should part and my brilliant insights should break through the gloom and offer peace and perspective. *Hmmm* . . . ? Here's what I've got: I suspect depending on our specific storyline, each point of view poses challenges, but whichever outlook gets us over the hump is the route to take. If you find that forgiving someone is too arduous, then focus your attention on acceptance and vice versa. Because in the end holding onto resentment, anger and nurturing the injustices of our past only deprive us of savoring the adventure of our lives.

Do we really want to spend the precious opportunities our short life affords us by stewing and blaming? I do not. And I suggest we use whatever means at our disposal to get us to a place of contentment and appreciation in spite of the horrors and quirks of our individual narrative.

Forgiveness or acceptance is always going to be an uphill slog, but everything of true value takes hard work. It's hard to learn to speak a foreign language or play a musical instrument, have a successful marriage or raise happy children. However, if we are willing to keep climbing—like scaling a mountain—there is a breathtaking view awaiting us: that glorious moment when you speak French in a Parisian bistro, or flawlessly play that Chopin sonata, or watch your child put on a graduation cap and gown.

It's never easy getting to the top of the mountain, but once you're there . . . it's all downhill!

> *We all have our baggage, and I think the trick is not resisting it but accepting it, understanding that the worst experience has a valuable gift wrapped inside if you're willing to receive it.*
> —Jeannette Walls,
> *The New York Times Magazine*

Day 17

Starving

May 31, 2013

I'M STARVING!

No, I mean it, I am always hungry. And the unimaginably cruel truth is that when I was a child I never really cared that much about food. When I think of all the cheeseburgers, fried chicken, ice cream and French fries I consumed as a child . . . and with never a thought of calorie intake or fat content or cholesterol consequences. Free to eat myself into a junk food coma if I so desired. How wonderful to be blithely unaware that the gravy train would someday come to a screeching halt, and I would one sad day be looking at a rice cake as my tragic evening snack!

While I have no background in psychology, I am acutely aware that my bottomless pit is reflective of all manner of hungers. I believe we are all hungry: hungry for healing, for understanding, for encouragement and for companionship. Mostly, I think we are hungry for God.

We tell ourselves that we hunger for more money, more security, more affection, more food; but in actuality, what we are craving is that presence of the Divine. We are famished for belief that our life has significance and that a supernatural encounter with wisdom, beauty and fulfillment is possible. It does not take a remarkable amount of materialism or self-indulgence to acknowledge the unfulfilling nature of these goals.

The Catholic tradition that I work and minister within will be proclaiming the story of Jesus multiplying the loaves and fishes this Sunday. Many of the significant biblical stories involve food and Jesus' concern that those around him be fed. At the end of his ministry when describing himself, he does not use a financial or military metaphor, he says, *"I am bread, I am wine." "I am food and I am drink."* And just as we need nourishment and hydration to stay alive, so too, we need the Holy.

This journal entry was inspired by an editorial I read in the *New York Times* on Wednesday by T. M. Luhrmann, where she explores the distinction between "belief" and church attendance.[1] Luhrmann writes, *"God is good. The world is good. Things will be good, even if they don't seem good now. That's what draws people to church. It is understandably hard for secular observers to sidestep the problem of belief. But it is worth appreciating that in belief is the reach for joy, and the reason many people go to church in the first place."*

I agree that we go to church in spite of the multiplicity of our beliefs but also that in church—in the communal silences, in the recitation of ancient prayers, in the congregational singing—we finally experience fullness, completion, answers and questions and finally . . . an occasional breathtaking encounter with our loving and forgiving God. What are you hungry for when you go to church? What happens there that satisfies you? Tell me.

Day 18

Summertime

June 4, 2013

Summer's warmth and light infuse
the fruits of the earth with rich colors,
varied texture and deep fragrance.
You bring bread from the earth
and wine to gladden our hearts.
*   —Psalm 104*

I LOVE SUMMERTIME. Or maybe I just love the *idea* of summertime. I have such fond childhood memories of this season. Long unstructured days reading books and listening to the radio, playing record albums on a phonograph and having no responsibilities, other than occasionally mowing the lawn and taking out the garbage. A good amount of my young life was spent in the furnace of the Arizona desert, and while my family never owned a personal swimming pool, we always had friends and neighbors who did. For many years in Phoenix, those sizzling afternoons were spent at my best friend's backyard oasis. We would splash, swim and then lap water onto the concrete surround and bake on the pavement until crisp, rolling leisurely back into the cool, buoyant, underwater world.

I suppose at the heart of the summertime memories is the image of my life without responsibilities. No impossible messages to answer, no worries about money or the future, no dire decisions to be made: just get up when you desire, make your bed, have some breakfast and drift through an uncomplicated day in shorts and sandals. Will life ever be like that again? Or is it enough to have had it once? Like a painting one once owned and had to sell but is still treasured and remembered.

As I am growing older I have a sharpened hunger for that "idea" of summer and have found it necessary to uncomplicate and unclutter my life as much as possible so as to recapture a fragment of that emptiness. Because in that freedom is an awareness of the texture of the moment. This moment. The moment in which I am listening—truly listening to the person in front of me and not glancing at my watch with anxiety about the time of my next appointment. The holy moment, when I watch the fog clutch at the mountain peaks of the city where I live. The evening moment, when I stop preparations for bed and thank my God for the gift of the day and listen to the sweet, quiet sounds of the night outside my bedroom window. The smallest moments of every day, when I recognize the blessings that surround me even in challenge, sorrow and loneliness. In simplifying my life, I have made room for God. And I believe I can feel that loving, tolling, eternal presence; it is as tangible as the sun on my face in the dream of my childhood summers.

> *Summer afternoon—summer afternoon; to me those have always been the two most beautiful words in the English language.*
> –Henry James

Day 19

Reinventing

June 7, 2013

> *As he was walking along the Sea of Galilee,*
> *he watched two brothers,*
> *Simon, now known as Peter, and his brother*
> *Andrew, casting a net into the sea.*
> *They were fisherman.*
> *He said to them, "Come after me and I will make*
> *you fishers of men."*
> *They immediately abandoned their nets and*
> *became his followers.*
>
> –Matthew 4:18–20

I NEVER LEARNED TO COOK. It's almost embarrassing to admit. Like acknowledging you need assistance in some simple task like tying a shoelace, operating a washing machine or . . . steaming

49

vegetables. The ugly truth is that at a time in my life when I would have naturally begun to experiment with cooking food, I went to the seminary and we ate every meal in a refectory. After my ordination I was assigned to a large church with a cook. And after that, well, cooking became a mountain too daunting to scale. Recently I had dinner at the home of some friends and invited them back to my parish apartment to watch a movie and have dessert purchased at a local bakery (*as if you needed THAT clarification*) and while waiting for the tea my friend noticed a cookbook on the counter displayed for decoration purposes only and suggested we make a date and prepare a dish from the cookbook! "COOK? PREPARE RAW FOOD? ME? NO!" Immediately my mind flooded with objections and excuses, I had cinematic images of dirty pots and pans, scalded fingertips and the most horrific vision of them all: failure.

Why are we so afraid to try something new? I'll tell you why: the possibility of failure. Eleonora Sharef is quoted in a recent *New York Times* editorial by Thomas Friedman who is writing about what employers desire in job applicants: *"The most successful job candidates, she added, are 'inventors and solution-finders,' who are relentlessly 'entrepreneurial' because they understand that many employers today don't care about your resumé, degree or how you got your knowledge, but only what you can do and what you can continuously reinvent yourself to do."*[1]

This idea of "reinvention" is intriguing to me because I suspect it is a crucial survival tool. Crucial and terrifying because if we are willing to reinvent our carefully constructed and preserved personalities, we might fail. Most people I know define themselves at some life juncture and never make a course correction. But is that not what conversion is all about? Change? The willingness to relentlessly reinvent who we have become; to discard that which is petty, narrow-minded, grumpy and self-righteous.

When Jesus gathered his followers, he would call them and with no interest whatsoever in their past, he asked simply, *"Will you follow me?"* Will you leave behind your routine, familiarity and presumed safety and join me in a great cosmic undertaking? Will you stop fishing and tax collecting and reinvent yourself in an adventure that will be perceived by the people of this age as a monumental failure? I believe God, like the modern-day employers in the New York Times quote above, is uninterested in our past and in our failures, but rather, fascinated with our willingness to use this great gift of life for inventing and reinventing who we can become every day.

DAY 20

Attention Please

June 11, 2013

The first duty of love is to listen.
–Paul Tillich

IN 1993, BILL MOYERS presented a five-part series on Public Broadcasting entitled "Healing and the Mind." It was an exploration into holistic healing which took the viewers outside the traditional western approach to medicine. The final episode of the series took place in a retreat house in Bolinas, California, where terminal cancer patients could spend a week receiving physical therapies, walk along the shore and enter into group discussions with the other participants.

At the beginning of the group session, the facilitator, Dr. Rachel N. Remen, explained that each person in the circle would have a chance to tell their story and the others would listen uninterruptedly until each speaker concluded. She said, "We will not interrupt or ask questions, we will simply listen . . . because the most generous gift we can give another person is our *undivided attention.*"

Undivided attention. What a beautiful phrase. And what a luxury. It feels akin to gazing into a jewelry store window at a breathtakingly, unattainable object! I could commence here with a screed about technology and how it has splintered our ability to concentrate, however, that might be a smidge disingenuous coming from a man whose beloved iPhone never leaves his side for an instant. Rather, let me say that when I am in conversation with someone who gives me the lavish gift of their absorption, I feel blessed; I feel heard; I feel that I am being respected and appreciated. On the other hand, when the person with whom I am in conversation is staring determinedly at a gadget or looking over and around me to see who just entered the room, I feel diminishment. It requires a certain discipline in this modern world to sharpen our attention upon the human beings surrounding us. It means training the wandering mind to focus on one single thing.

What "out there" is more important than the person right in front of us? So many people make excuses *(including the writer of Journal of a Country Priest)* for being distracted: multiple responsibilities, weariness, the absolute vital nature of everything surrounding me. However, how can we expect others to listen to us when we ourselves exhibit supreme unwillingness to stop all the activity, take a deep breath and attend to the here and now? I have a deeply held suspicion that whatever we are looking for on the phone, in the tablet or around the next corner is actually right in front of us, just waiting for us to finally see the light.

> *Too often we underestimate the power of a touch,*
> *a smile, a kind word, a listening ear, an honest*
> *compliment, or the smallest act of caring, all of*
> *which have the potential to turn a life around.*
> –Leo F. Buscaglia

Day 21

Possibilities

June 14, 2013

> *. . . for nothing is impossible with God.*
>
> *–Luke 1*

M ANY YEARS AGO, I was returning from a visit to my parents with an elderly nun friend of mine named Sister Angela. On the way to the airport, there had been some kind of altercation between my father and me. Sitting on the plane with my friend, I was fuming. My father and I shared a very bad trait: our brand of anger is self-perpetuating. I was systematically constructing a vortex of fury, blindness and despair. Sister Angela calmly looked at me and said, *"You must take this to God because it is too big for you, but it's not too big for God."* That sentence changed my life. "It's too big for you, but it's not too big for God."

I know, I know—I can envision the expression of skepticism on the faces of some of my friends. And I myself hate trite, inspirational phrases, but something about the idea behind her words has brought me enormous peace over the years. I suppose this expression is related to the concept of the infinite possibilities of God. I am always preaching about God's infinite possibilities and getting blank looks from congregations. Nevertheless, I keep pitching that ball into the park because it thrills me. It is exciting to consider that when we have exhausted our resources, when no more solutions seem viable, when every door is slammed shut, something unexpected might happen.

Have you never been in a situation when your circumstances appeared hopeless—when your imagination and ingenuity were stumped? And suddenly something wonderful happens? Something that you never considered unfurls and takes your breath away? Oh, I'll bet it has. Stop shaking your head from side to side!

Being a believer is trusting that the Creator, the Father, the Intelligent Designer—whoever you imagine God to be—can envision solutions and outcomes that surpass our imaginings. Like a child that presumes the parent will protect and provide without being able to grasp how that remarkable reality will occur, so we consider our Higher Power will take that which seems unsolvable and create solutions, resolutions, healings, fulfillments, rainfalls, harvests, romances, joys and weave them all into the story of our lives so that we are saved.

Still shaking your head? Well, maybe this is all a bit too big for you, *but...*

Day 22

Making Music

June 18, 2013

> *God has done great things for us*
> *filled us with laughter and music.*
> —Marty Haugen, Psalm 126

I HAVE BEEN SPOILED MY ENTIRE LIFE with access to music. There were always radios, record players, cassettes, eight-track players, CDs, and now Pods and Pads creating soundtracks to accompany my many moods! Music has always been in my family, and I was even given the gift of piano lessons when I was a child—lessons with a wonderful teacher who loved children and wanted them to be excited about making music. However, in my infinite nine-year-old wisdom, I walked away from that opportunity because I did not want to practice. And like millions before and undoubtedly after me, I regret surrendering that phenomenal opportunity. Consequently, one of my life's goals is to finally learn to play the piano.

There is something mysterious and indescribably beautiful about the piano. The shape of the instrument's body, the arranged ivory and black keys, the variation of sound from whispering to a roar, all combine into a complete seduction. Imagine being able to sit in front of that magnificent object and make music. "Make music," not "plug in" or "turn on" but *make* that extraordinary sound that moves, inspires, stirs and romances.

Don't you weep at the movie because of the music? Imagine your daughter floating down the church aisle in a white dress without music! The marching band on the playing field, the song at your first school dance, James Taylor singing *You've Got a Friend*, Judy Garland's *Over the Rainbow,* or Joan Sutherland rocking the chandeliers at the Sydney Opera House.

That all sounds so romantic doesn't it? The reality of beginning to play a musical instrument is not very romantic at all. All those inspirational images boil down to getting up very early in the morning and creeping resentfully into a stone-cold church and attempting the seemingly impossible: to somehow make my awkward and clumsy fingers do what a piece of sheet music is (*rather smugly*) telling me to do. "FORTE!" "PIANISSIMO!" "SCALES!" And now, horrifyingly, one hand playing one line of music while the other hand plays another at the same time! Madness! And yet everything, and I do mean everything, of any true value comes with hard work: a happy marriage, an academic degree, fluency with a foreign language and the chocolate soufflé.

So let's keep practicing and together we will find a way to make beautiful music.

> *If music be the food of love, play on!*
> *–Shakespeare's Twelfth Night*

Day 23

Gridlock!

June 21, 2013

FOR MANY YEARS I lived in a northern coastal region that was equally beautiful to the landscape I currently inhabit, however that area was frequently choked with traffic! Is there anything more frustrating? You're sailing along with a full agenda of appointments and responsibilities and you jump into an onramp and *screech* to a depressing stop. You are trapped. Gridlocked. And there is no way out. I've never been able to discern whether it is worse to be at a dead standstill or inching painstakingly forward. Either condition is excruciating for now you know that you will be late. Your whole day will not be in sync, and the consequences of this torture begin to reverberate within, until you become a simmering, anxious wreck.

The place where I now live is almost traffic free. Oh there are those moments when you get behind a slow-moving truck or road construction bottlenecks three lanes into one, but for the most part, I zoom across this map. Last night I was invited to the country home of a parishioner and was making my way there at a time of day when people all over the planet were undoubtedly stationary. I was zipping through mountains, vineyards, ordered sections of earth designated for gigantic heads of red cabbage and this entire splendor sitting placidly under a windswept slate blue sky. In moments like those, I am suffused with gratitude for the ability to move unencumbered: to be able to dash here and there without getting stuck! I cannot help but wonder if my heart and soul are as free as the traffic patterns in this Utopia.

It occurs to me that Jesus is always offering freedom and forgiveness. His voice is always calling us to look at this current moment and beyond. In my own life there have been great, precious volumes of time spent brooding over the past: decisions, injustices, heartbreaks that have paralyzed and crippled my ability to be happy or optimistic.

And I am not alone. Conversations with others frequently revolve around their inability to release the past or make peace with the present. I am not sure precisely how one lets go of those ancient wounds and emotional traffic jams, but it seems that the first step is to direct your vehicle to the off-ramp.

To desire freedom is the beginning of an amazing journey that takes you out of the prison of yesterday and into the free moving world of the possible.

> *The secret of happiness is freedom, the secret of*
> *freedom is courage.*
> —Carrie Jones, *Need*

DAY 24

CЗ

Summer Movie Love

June 25, 2013

MY EARLIEST MEMORY OF GOING TO A MOVIE occurred when I was five years old. My mother took me to see *Mary Poppins*. I remember vividly that I was wearing a tweed coat and a matching cap and when I sat in front of the car, my legs did not wrap around the seat but rather stuck out straight. I don't remember being told about the film or if the experience was a treat for good behavior. I just remember sitting down in the darkened theatre and this unanticipated magic unfolded before my eyes. That was the beginning of a passionate love that changed my life forever.

There are cinematic moments that seem more real to me than my actual experience of living. I'm always amazed when I meet someone who never watches movies or television because these images have so profoundly influenced my choices and behavior.

I still remember a time when a curtain would rise over the screen. I still remember the occasional intermission in the midst of particularly long movie. What is there about sitting in a darkened room with a group of strangers while a story unfurls that is so compelling? I love those moments when everyone jumps simultaneously in a thriller, or weeps at a death scene, or relaxes after a long battle. It feels like unimaginable luxury to be transported safely to Istanbul or an African safari or a loft apartment in Greenwich Village without waiting in an interminable airport security line or worrying about the drinking water.

James Bond, Scarlett O'Hara, Julia Roberts or Tom Hanks would never ask impertinent questions or bore me with too many personal demands. And while they are merely the light and shadow of science and art, they have brought me insight, hope and courage. On occasion I have left movie theatres with renewed energy and fresh perspective. I am grateful to sit in a comfortable chair, eat hot buttered popcorn and have a battalion of unseen technicians tell me a story for two hours. While I must admit I rarely go out to a movie theatre these days, I look forward to the next ride—the next movie that gets my pulse twitching or my eyes watering or my heart breaking. And you: what are the movies that have stirred your soul and shaken your core?

Day 25

The Prophet is False

June 28, 2013

> *Jesus said to his disciples:*
> *"Beware of false prophets,*
> *who come to you in sheep's clothing,*
> *but underneath are ravenous wolves."*
> –Matthew 7

MANY YEARS AGO, I WAS ATTENDING a Catholic parish that featured an extremely charismatic priest. He spoke with remarkable passion and an almost uncanny ability to tap into the collective unconscious of the listening public. He was tremendously inspirational and possessed the enviable ability to ferociously challenge the assembly without driving us out the door! He was able to bridge the past with the present and could translate very old ideas and theology into fresh and vibrant sound bites. However, in time after the initial sparkle had begun to dull, I found myself analyzing some of his content with dismay. It occurred to me that he was actually twisting the Jesus message to support various political agendas.

After twenty-five years of studying and interpreting the Jesus story, I keep returning to his consistent message of inclusion, compassion and love. Consider the encounter Jesus has with the marginalized: there is always acceptance and affirmation for their faith. He rewards people for their ability to look beyond the current thinking and their willingness to glimpse the possibilities for a new interpretation of God's identity and ultimately God's desire for the human family. Be honest, when you listen to the images and stories in the Bible don't you hear an echo of God's priority for human beings to love, honor and forgive one another? Is there not an unwavering yearning for us to love God, neighbor and self? How then does that on-point communication turn into interpretations of *exclusion* and judgment?

Believe me: I, like everyone else in the world, can get seduced by eloquence, fervor and physical beauty. Like all people, I love nothing more than hearing an inspired person verbalize and confirm my own personal and political inclinations. Nevertheless, if what I am hearing in church is not inspiring me to reach for a more profoundly loving relationship with my mysterious God, if it is not propelling me into forgiving my neighbors and the stranger, if my self-esteem and self-confidence are not improving with the preaching, then I need to *move on*! And so must you. Because the false prophet will accomplish the complete opposite of our heart's desire. The false prophet makes us angry and the true prophet brings us peace.

> *"Teacher, what must I do to inherit ever-*
> *lasting life?"*
> *Jesus answered him: "What is written in the law?*
> *How do you read it?"*
> *He replied: "You shall love the Lord your God with*
> *all your heart,*
> *with all your soul, with all your strength,*
> *and with all your mind;*
> *and your neighbor as yourself."*
> *Jesus said, "You have answered correctly. Do this*
> *and you shall live."*
>
> –Luke 10:25-37

DAY 26

I'm "Leaning"

July 2, 2013

SHERYL SANDBERG, THE FACEBOOK DYNAMO, recently published a book with her ruminations on how women can become more successful in the world of business. Her ingenious title is *Lean In*. While I have not read the book, I did see a *60 Minutes* segment featuring her at the time of publication. I am struck by how alluring her title is and how deftly she tapped into the zeitgeist of the moment. From listening to her interview, I believe she is proposing that women lean into more business responsibility, lean into a greater acceptance of work/home lifestyle compromises, and lean into a new identity of self-confidence and decision making.

I'm intrigued by all this "leaning." Since the publication of her book, I see and hear that word everywhere. This morning on the elliptical machine at the gym the political program on the flat screen was titled "Lean Forward." Leaning is peppering conversations, the written word and graduation speeches at colleges and universities.

Why all this leaning? I suspect because it suggests a less intrusive, less vulnerable way of entering into a situation or circumstance. It feels less confrontational than a full attack. Anything that allows us to take temperatures and acquire samples before commitment is appealing to this generation. We don't fire employees; we lean into a conversation that begins to indicate that their work is coming to an end. We don't propose marriage; we lean into an understanding that gradually becomes an agreement. We don't announce a specific goal; we discern our general objectives and allow the specifics to be shaped by the unpredictable. All of this feels to me like a roundabout way of avoiding the hideous possibility of failure.

Once we state our desire we have made a pledge that may or may not succeed. But if we allude, suggest and lean, then our advancement or diminishment might not be readily apparent to the critical observer. We might even be able to evade perceiving ourselves as having failed.

Don't get me wrong; I like the lean. I like assessing, studying, smoke screening, but eventually, we have to make the jump. At some point, we must purchase the house, discipline the child, and accept the consequences of our losses or winnings.

Ultimately, someone has to say the words, *"I love you,"* *"I forgive you,"* or *"I'll take care of you."* If we keep angling ourselves in and out, at some juncture the lean becomes a push or a fall into the outcome. And the magic trick is finding a way to accept with dignity and contentment the inevitable rise and fall of our life story.

Day 27

Haunting

July 9, 2013

HAVING RETURNED FROM A WEEK IN NEW YORK CITY, I am obsessed with all things NYC. So I watched Martin Scorsese's *The Age of Innocence*. The movie is his translation of the Edith Wharton novel. It is beautifully stylized cinema with magnificent costumes and rigidly authentic settings. The story depicts a time in which the presentation of impeccable sexual morality was imperative for those seeking acceptance in the upper echelons of New York society. The main character, Newland Archer, is a refined gentleman in love with an exceedingly well-bred girl, who has a spotless reputation. It is to be a brilliant marriage that becomes sullied when he meets a cousin of his fiancée who is in the midst of a scandalous divorce. He is dazzled by this woman's wit, beauty and unconventionality. And while they are tremendously attracted to each other, ultimately she departs for Paris and he to his expected role of loving husband and father. At the end of the movie, he has the opportunity to meet the object of his obsession after many years, and he chooses instead to walk away and allow the memory of his love for her to remain in the past. It is a heartbreaking scene full of layers of intention and meaning.

After viewing the film, I was reminded of a quote attributed to Plato in which he wrote, "Be kind. For everyone you meet is in the midst of a great battle." *The Age of Innocence* becomes the story of a man who lives his life with a great regret that he could never have the woman he loved. And yet, even in the midst of his sorrow, he raised a family, earned a living, contributed to the betterment of his community and attempted to be a loving, faithful man.

I wonder how many people we see every day carry some great pain or suffering never spoken of? How many people do we pass in the street or interface with in a store or a restaurant who are awaiting a diagnosis, or who are in the midst of declaring bankruptcy, or have been rejected by a lover or spouse? How many have no idea where their children are or if they will ever see them again?

When we carry sorrow or disappointment, it takes remarkable courage to soldier on without self-pity. And I cannot help but wonder if everyone is haunted by that one significant individual from the past. What if everyone has someone who was loved and lost—the person we still consider when the morning coffee is cooling or daydream about in a lengthy traffic jam? The individual who was impossibly difficult or ambivalent or deceased.

The person who drifts across your consciousness just before slumber or when desperately unhappy or lonely. The *One* who our imagination assumes would never be boorish or selfish. The *One* in which our true happiness would have been realized. If everyone has such a person longed for and never revealed, doesn't that give us yet another reason to extend a little extra patience and understanding to all engaging in this ongoing battle?

> *There's always someone haunting someone*
> *And I can't sleep easy*
> *'Cause I'm afraid of dreaming*
> *And then there's the memory of the dream*
> *There's always someone haunting someone*
> *Haunting someone*
> *Haunting someone.*
> –Carly Simon, *Haunting*

DAY 28

∝

Bookworm

July 16, 2013

I have always imagined that Paradise will be a kind
of library.
> –Jorge Louis Borges

WOULD MAKE A LOUSY DETECTIVE. Were I to witness a crime, I suspect I would never be able to recount the details to the police. However, I love reading detective stories and mysteries. Long ago I figured out that in spite of the fact that I never accurately identify the evildoer and am sometimes confused by the specifics of the plot, I love the repeated experience of being absorbed in a story where the characters are gradually accumulating information and enlightenment. I often think that the spiritual person is a kind of detective: God leaves us clues and when we study nature and human behavior, when we engage in prayer and celebration of the sacraments, we slowly begin to uncover the mystery of God.

It occurs to me that one of the enduring passions of my life is a love of books. I can spend hours in a bookstore or library and consider places where books are sold or loaned to be sacred spaces. I recently made a trip to New York City and visited for the first time the New York Public Library and had my photograph taken in front of it, the way some people pose beside the Grand Canyon or Eiffel Tower!

Although I inhabit a world where the gradual acquisition of knowledge has been replaced by the need for immediate, paperless information, I continue to revere the experience of a bound text. There is something almost indescribable about the heft, smell and texture of reading an actual book. The subtle pleasures of reading include the rustling of the pages, the transportation to a dreamlike state, the satisfaction of finishing a challenging story, or the reluctant placing of a bookmark within the spine so one can return to the exact spot. All these moments are akin to oxygen for the bookworm.

I personally have no desire to scale Everest, or bust up a drug cartel or be rejected by the love of my life, but the experience of reading allows me to safely enter these worlds and return to my own life enriched, entertained and expanded.

What are you reading this summer? What are the books and stories that have changed your life or shifted your perspective? What is the book you would give as a gift?

"A reader lives a thousand lives before he dies,"
said Jojen. "The man who never reads lives only
once."

–George R. R. Martin,
A Dance with Dragons

Day 29

Church

July 20, 2013

I WATCHED A LIGHTLY ENTERTAINING MOVIE on cable recently, entitled *Salmon Fishing in the Yemen*. It is an unusual romantic comedy with a somewhat unpredictable storyline, but at one point in the film, there is dialog between the two main characters in which they agree to a business meeting on Sunday. The man presumes the woman would not be going to church on Sunday since "*. . . nobody I know goes to church anymore. My wife and I go to Target on Sunday!*" It was meant as a soft, humorous aside, not a full-blown joke. Nevertheless, comments like that sting. As a pastor who works very hard to make the Sunday experience the best it can be, I feel comments like that in real or reel life somehow give permission for people to identify church attendance as antediluvian. When one enters into conversations with people about why they no longer attend church, they will present a platter of reasons: they are busy, tired, overextended, overcommitted, stressed, and the ultimate and most devastating complaint, church is boring.

When did boredom become the unforgivable sin? How did we evolve into a culture who simply cannot bear to be in a state of non-stimulation at all times? Certainly, I could respond to my question by examining the effects of television and the internet, both of which provide a never-ending platform for excitement, diversion and distraction. However, it feels more layered than just that. It would appear to me that we are existing in an environment where a lengthy explanation or silent reflection, pondering, wondering and considering is becoming intolerable. And those aforementioned qualities are the very essence of a fulfilling worship experience. Church is about the gathering of people who have questions, longings, joys, anxieties, hungers and needs. And when we sing together or sit together in silence or listen to sacred texts together there is something undefinable that happens to the human soul. On occasion, I have practically stomped into my church in a wretched temper only to have the personalities, music, and atmosphere wash over and heal me like medicine. I was once in the pew of a church in New York City where at the end of a long, rather rambling homily, I felt tears rolling down my face from the relief and encouragement I felt at the end of the message.

If I think about going to the gym, I am never excited—running nowhere on a treadmill? Lifting heavy and dangerous weights above my head? Sweating? Straining? *Booorrrring!* But after I walk away from that effort there is a kind of euphoria that remains with me throughout the day. Consequently, I believe the effort one makes to leave everyday life and enter into sacred time and space with an assembly of searching people will reward us gradually in ways that are not necessarily immediately stimulating.

This kind of plea is akin to rearranging the deck chairs on the *Titanic*; nevertheless, I want to send out a tiny flare of warning: There are treacherous icebergs ahead if we seek only that which is expedient or convenient. And I wish to lure you in with the promise of transcendence on that unexpected Sunday morning when the silence or the words to the hymn or the homily slam into your heart and reverberate the message: you are not alone!

DAY 30

Time Travel

July 26, 2013

THERE IS SOMETHING MAGICAL about a photo album. Have you noticed that when you sit down and begin to turn the pages of a family scrapbook, the world falls away and you are transported to another place? It feels like time travel. Everything vanishes and suddenly there is your childhood home, you in school uniform on your first day at Saint Peter and Paul, and here you are holding a Little League bat and there again blowing out birthday cake candles and always the eyes captured wide with excitement. More amazing still are the images of ancestors: grandparents and uncles, aunts and parents posing in military uniforms, in front of Christmas trees and wearing wedding gowns glowing from the past in surprisingly current eyewear.

My mother is recently widowed. While staying with her

for a few summer weeks, one of my projects is to go through containers of old family photographs and begin some kind of organization process. I open a musty box and suddenly there, wrapped in disintegrating tissue paper, is a photograph of my great-grandfather in military regalia. Here, my grandmother's travel journal from her honeymoon trip to Niagara Falls; there, a letter written by a woman my godfather fell in love with during the war and who did not wait for him; and everywhere, postcards from Santa Fe, Lake Louise, and the Hawaiian Islands.

As I unearth this buried treasure, my mother tells me stories of these people whose blood runs through my veins but who are virtual strangers to me. She struggles to recall the specifics of their romances, heartbreaks, diseases and triumphs.

The ghosts leave behind only fading paper. Their passions, bankbooks, adventures are all gone. I wonder about the brevity of human life and the extraordinary amounts of time we spend in anxiety. How often do we miss the sunset, the ice cream or the music because we want it all to be different, better or more? How frequently do we nourish the grudge, regret the past or attempt to control the future? Has anyone ever really harnessed the future? (*And if so, who are they? And where can I find their Twitter?*)

What if in the end, that which is significant are the moments we were truly honest with others and ourselves? Is it possible that the only eternal possessions in this life are the prayers, the dancing, the cheering at the home runs, the singing and the moments we actually said the words, "*I love you.*" What if long after our stories are forgotten, the only thing that remains is our love, the generosity and our open heart? And everything else . . . *just fades away.*

Day 31

Things

August 4, 2013

Think of what is above, not of what is on earth.
–Saint Paul to the Colossians

YEARS AGO, I VISITED SANTA FE, NEW MEXICO and went into a gallery where there was an exquisite glass bowl displayed under a spotlight. It was actually ceramic but made to look like crystal. Paint was washed across the sides like watercolor and the effect was brilliant. I had to have it! At the time it seemed terribly expensive, but something about it called to me and I impulsively purchased the bowl. In the beginning, it was my treasure and occupied a place of great pride in the center of wherever I lived. However, gradually I began to take it for granted as another object that needed to be dusted and cared for. Its beauty and uniqueness began to have less significance. Over the years, it was admired by many of my acquaintances, and once I had the opportunity of returning a favor by gifting the bowl to a generous friend but decided against it. I now have no idea where that vessel is. In the past years I have moved several times and have lost track of its whereabouts; perhaps it is wrapped safely in a bin or smashed into a million slivers inside a box. Regardless, its enchantment has worn off and the opportunity to experience generosity with something precious may be forever lost.

This weekend's scripture readings are warning me against materialism and indicating fulfillment is to be found in kindness, generosity, patience and faithfulness. I have come to a place in my life where I finally believe this to be true. For many years I was entranced by beautiful things and believed them to possess great power. What I have learned is that something beautiful or desired may distract for a time, but after the initial thrill has worn off, it is still necessary to put gasoline in the car, practice the piano, return the phone call, sort through the mail and perform a gazillion other tedious and necessary tasks. The object of my desire does not transform my existence, but sometimes actually adds to the burden of it. I find myself eager to eliminate everything I am not utilizing or needing so that I can experience the maximum freedom of and attentiveness to that which is important to me.

And what is important to me today? What has become essential is to be able to savor and appreciate nature: the smell and sight of the morning as its light creeps across the dome of the sky. To halt in my myriad of tasks and listen to the sound of the wind, the rain or the wildlife. To telephone my mother every day and memorize the sound of her voice as she speaks. To read books and digest new ideas. To attempt mastery of a musical instrument. To broaden the quality and quantity of my friendships, and to spend as much time as possible in the state of mirth. Because in the end, who cares about a bowl, or a diamond, or a piece of land? In the end, what matters is the way my father enfolded me in his embrace, the way the music made me weep at the concert and the number of times I say and receive the words, "*I love you.*"

In the end, these are the things that will remain.

Day 32

God's Dream

August 9, 2013

Faith is the realization of what is hoped for and evidence of things not seen.
—Hebrews 11:1

THERE ARE CERTAIN MOVIES I watch over and over because I want to live in the world of the film. One such movie is a romantic comedy called *You've Got Mail*. It's the story of an internet romance between two business adversaries. I re-watch it because it's a Hollywood fantasy of life in New York City. The main character, played by the actress Meg Ryan, has a scene in which she breaks up with her boyfriend, and in their conversation, he asks if she has someone else. She replies, *"No, but there is the dream of someone else."*

In my life, I frequently connect with people who have no faith. I am mystified by such individuals and wonder how they hold themselves together in the uphill climb of life. How does one face a diagnosis? Or injustice? What flickers through your mind as you are being wheeled into surgery? Where does such a person go when terrorists fly airplanes into the side of buildings? For whom do you reach when your spouse rejects you?

"Faith is the realization of what is hoped for and evidence of things not seen." This quote in Sunday's second reading is the author's beginning of instructing the Hebrews in the extraordinary faith had by Abraham, who was willing to sacrifice his son and leave his home. Abraham had a dream of a wise and loving God in whom anything is possible, and his faith made sense of all that was mysterious and unknowable.

Imagine if the world was a dream had by God. A God who teaches us fearlessness, goodness and equality. Faith is the knowledge of this powerful dream. And religion offers us the tools to decode the dream. When we have faith, we are connected to a tradition that believes somehow everything will work out and offers us prayers, gestures and community who provide comfort and balance when we are terrified or at peace. We often become preoccupied with the details of our lives and the cycles of happiness and disappointment, but when we are weary, when we are shattered, and even when we are triumphant—there is the dream. And the dream is a portal that enables us to glimpse what is unimaginable, and what is unimaginable is the splendor of God.

Day 33

Yesterday or Tomorrow?

August 13, 2013

*M*ESSAGE IN A BOTTLE is a wonderfully mystical movie about a woman who finds a bottle while running on a beach. Inside is a love letter from a man to a woman. The letter is a kind of romantic masterpiece stirring the woman so intensely she begins a quest to identify the writer. When she finally locates him, she finds a broken man grieving for the loss of his wife who died tragically some years before. He cannot imagine a life with someone new and will not let go of the past. In the dramatic, high point of the film, the man's father challenges his son to choose: *"Choose between yesterday and tomorrow and stay with it."*

Personally, I have found it very difficult to let go of the past. Not that there is anything especially unforgivable or unrepairable in my journey. It's just that in those moments when I am alone, empty or indecisive, it seems easier to replay and obsess over all that has gone before. My mind loves to relive crucial life scenes and shift them around until they create a more satisfactory outcome. I recently had a conversation with a colleague who told me he never looks back, and I was filled with envy. Imagine never looking back? How does one acquire that blissful state of mind? Christianity is absolutely about living in the perfect now moment, and the person of Jesus is eager to extend forgiveness and almost always ends his encounters with the directive to move on.

I wish I had the answer or the prayer or the therapist who could impart the secret to letting go of the past. This is all I know: The more I strive to be the person God made me—not who others tell me I *should* be—the efforts made towards speaking my truth, engaging with what truly inspires, is enabling me to create my best possible life story. And in savoring the beauty of where I live, in having work that challenges and inspires me, in cultivating friendships that serve up a feast of laughter and passion, I find that day-by-day I am creating a more compelling 'now' than the familiar reruns of the past.

> *Whoever puts a hand to the plow but keeps*
> *looking back is unfit for the reign of God.*
>   *–Luke*

Day 34

Dreaming of My Father

August 16, 2013

'It shall come to pass in the last days,' says God,
'That I will pour out a portion of my spirit
on all humankind.
Your sons and daughters shall prophesy,
Your young men shall see visions,
your old men shall dream dreams.
　　　–Acts 2:17

LAST NIGHT I HAD A DREAM of my father. He was young, strong and carrying me on his shoulders so that I could see what is above. It was a wonderful vision depicting a moment I have no memory of ever having lived through. My father died somewhat unexpectedly three months ago, and I find I am still processing that one of the great loves of my life is no longer here. I have a friend who lost her husband some years ago and she tells a story about how in the aftermath of his death she felt a rush of his presence physically move through her. She knew it was him and she felt a profound sensation of his love throughout her being. For some strange reason, I was convinced I would have a similar encounter when my father passed. He was a part of me; we shared intense physical and personal characteristics. He raised me, supported me, disciplined me and longed for my happiness and fulfillment. Surprisingly, when he died there was no sense of his presence, no supernatural events—none of the mystical encounters I assumed would be a component of his departure. And now a sliver of a dream has brought me such comfort.

The Bible is filled with examples of God using dreams and visions in order to communicate specific information or direct the course of human activity. However, despite being of a fairly fanciful nature, I have never had cosmic messages, or if I did, they turned out to be misinterpreted. I often wonder about the validity of such experiences; and yet, if they bring the recipient comfort and reassurance, who cares about the legitimacy of their origin. Perhaps we are designed with the ability to close our eyes, float into a sleep state and enter another realm of consciousness in order to envision the unimaginable, to encounter the unrealistic, to conceptualize what the mind rejects in the daylight.

In my spiritual tradition, we believe that we are in communion with the saints, and so is it not possible that those we love who have passed over continue to be connected to us in inexplicable ways? What if their communication with the living is limited to dreams, shadows, distant music and currents of air? Is it conceivable that in their lifetime they loved and protected us and in the next life continue to find ways to raise us up on their shoulders so we can see beyond the barriers of this life? I wonder if those we have loved and lost are always waiting . . . waiting to lift us up so we can see a greater view.

> Prospero:
> Our revels now are ended. These our actors, as
> I foretold you, were all spirits and are melted
> into air, into thin air. And like the baseless
> fabric of this vision, the cloud-capp'd tow'rs,
> the gorgeous palaces, the solemn temples, the
> great globe itself, Yea, all which it inherit, shall
> dissolve, and, like this insubstantial pageant
> faded, leave not a rack behind. We are such
> stuff as dreams are made on, and our little life is
> rounded with a sleep.
> –The Tempest, Act 4,
> William Shakespeare

Day 35

Describing the Ghosts

August 20, 2013

S OME WEEKS AGO, I watched an old Sally Field movie called *Kiss Me Goodbye*. It was the lightest of material about a young widow returning to her house years after the death of her husband. The character has decided to marry and wants to redecorate the home and prepare for a new chapter. She is overwhelmed with memories of the perfect life she had shared with her husband and is eventually confronted by his ghost played by James Caan. Only she can see the spirit of her deceased husband, and their playful interaction causes her conflict about her choice of a fiancé. The story has a familiar trajectory with the main character having conversations with the ghost that no one else can see or hear, and just about the time you are reaching for the remote control, there is an interesting conclusion. The husband has come back not to remind her how splendid their marriage was, but rather to remind her that, although he was wonderful, he could also be tiresome and demanding and that she must finally *kiss him goodbye* in order to begin her new life free of past illusions. These ideas interest me—that we tend to idealize the dead and they continue to have the power to teach us life lessons.

In a few days, I am preparing to speak at the Memorial Mass for my father and find myself considering the aforementioned ideas. My first inclination is to describe him to the assembly in such a way that his humanity is obscured. It can easily be done with a description of his many virtues and authentic acts of charity. However, he was a completely human person with a full range of emotions, conflicts and blessings. The combination of these characteristics made him who he was: not a villain or hero but a marvelously complex and layered human being. I can't help but wonder if that truth causes all of us some consternation. We always want to be the good guy, the one who is always right, celebrated and successful. It appears to be difficult to swallow the possibility that we might be considered foolish, temperamental or flawed.

If the eulogy is a summation of our life, and if we are willing to express the full range of colors in the deceased's journey, can there be a greater acceptance of our humanity? Isn't that what makes us such interesting creatures? Our choices, detours and passions are what make us who we are. I have no desire to treasure the memory of who I *wanted* my father to be, rather I want to honor and remember who he really was and the unique story he lived. In this regard, he continues to inspire me and I suspect that inspiration will continue throughout my life even though he is gone.

> *You will weep and mourn while the world rejoices.*
> *You will grieve for a time but your tears will be*
> *turned into joy.*
> *When a woman is in labor she is sad that her time*
> *has come.*
> *When she has borne her child she no longer*
> *remembers her pain for joy that a human being has*
> *been born.*
> *In the same way, you are sad for a time but I shall*
> *see you again and your hearts will rejoice with a joy*
> *no one can take from you.*
> —John 16:19–22

Day 36

Restart

August 27, 2013

THE VERY FIRST COMPUTER I ever owned was a used Macintosh, purchased from a couple I was preparing for marriage. When it was acquired, I was actually unsure if I needed it. Now here I am, twenty-five years later, completely surrounded by smartphones, tablets, laptops and the "cloud." It is unimaginable making it through the day without these devices. While I am completely immersed in computer technology, I am not exactly sure how these machines function. However, in the world of Apple, I have learned one valuable lesson: when all else fails, "restart." A friend explained to me that as we ask these machines to perform a multitude of functions and as they jump here and there downloading, uploading, composing, responding, deleting, sorting and searching the World Wide Web, the insides tend to get gummed up. When you restart the device it clears the decks and repositions the mechanism for a fresh new beginning.

I often feel like those multitasking devices. Every day I find myself having to fracture my attention and operate on a multitude of levels: one moment celebrating the birth of an infant and the next offering consolation to the recently bereaved. I suspect our entire culture is attempting to exist on complex platforms, and we become lost in the jangling demands of everyday existence. Where is *that* restart command? How do we find that wonderful refresher that enables us to sweep away the confusion, the details, and the loss?

For me, I find that respite in prayer, laughter and in nature. It's true that there is something grounding in personal contemplative prayer, but also in the silence that can occur in church congregations. There is a marvelous moment created when everyone is quiet, still and the prayers rise in a perfectly focused moment.

Do you remember the last time you laughed out loud? Not the polite and appropriate titter that we incorporate into conversation but that belly laugh bursting out, shaking the frame and releasing the tension. The mirth that puts everything into perspective and enables us to see the world as a divine comedy. And then there is the beauty of the earth—just consider the light as it rises and falls at the beginning and ending of each day. I find the morning to be an especially sacred time—blurred illumination through the fog and on some brilliant days, the beginning of colors in the sky anticipating the emergence of the sun.

All of these moments are a natural form of restart for me and help me to reposition myself in the proper direction. It is impossible to imagine life without technology, but equally unimaginable is an existence without the sacred, every day manifested in beauty, laughter, friends, art and the holy conversation.

> *This city now doth, like a garment, wear*
> *the beauty of the morning; silent bare,*
> *ships, towers, domes, theatres and temples lie*
> *open unto fields and to the sky.*
> *All bright and glittering in the smokeless air.*
> *Never did sun more beautifully steep*
> *in his splendor, valley, rock or hill.*
> *Ne'er saw I, never felt, a calm so deep!*
> *The river glideth at his own sweet will.*
> *Dear God! The very houses seem asleep;*
> *And all that mighty heart is lying still!*
> 　　　　　–William Wordsworth

Day 37

Becoming

August 30, 2013

I RECENTLY CO-DIRECTED a weekend retreat for engaged couples. There must have been twenty of them—all young, self-confident and full of the knowledge necessary to rule the universe ... and sustain a happy marriage.

Remember that moment? You must. That glorious, deluded time when you actually believed you knew better than anyone how the world should be operating. That blissful clarity regarding finances, relationships, style, human interaction, child-rearing and God. What a wonderful time when you knew exactly what your parents should be doing, wearing, saying and how they should be voting. And not just parents but every other being on the planet earth. Sometimes it happens imperceptibly, and occasionally it's a battering ram, but life has a way of humbling us until the wretched day arrives when you're not really sure about whether you should be eating your breakfast cereal, much less how President Obama is running the United States!

One of the most difficult concepts to communicate to younger generations is how life changes us. Money or lack of it alters our everyday existence. Try explaining to a couple who are twenty-five that if you get hurt and spend every day in pain, this reality changes your personality. Having a child who is challenged in some way shifts everything and begins to dictate who your friends are and how your discretionary income is spent. Sickness, depression, addiction or the death of a family member can knock the wind out of us in such a devastating way that our self-confidence is shaken, and everything previously focused becomes blurred and unsteady.

The searing truth is we are all becoming something. That cranky next-door-neighbor did not pop out of the womb in a bad mood (well . . . maybe *he* did); undoubtedly, his experience of living ground away his optimism and goodwill. Without realizing it, he found himself, day-by-day, adopting a sour attitude until it became ingrained into his personality.

In my tradition, we have a spiritual exercise called "Examination of Conscience." This is the practice of reviewing our behavior and choices with the desire of removing those pesky elements that keep us from becoming the loving and generous people God intended. I cannot help but wonder if, before sleep, we all asked ourselves the question "What am I becoming?" Would the mere pondering of that query begin to redirect hostility, bitterness and spite? If we were aware that every encounter, each success and setback, is shaping and molding us, would we not become more attuned to what we hold onto and what we discard? Because for me, no matter what happens, I want to keep laughing, singing, praying, dreaming and creating until the day they put me in the earth.

And you? What are you becoming?

> *Examination of Conscience: a prayerful review*
> *of one's own life on the basis of gospel values.*
> *In the history of the Church, an examination of*
> *conscience has been part of spirituality from the*
> *earliest centuries. After Vatican II the examination*
> *of conscience, in the renewed rite of Penance, is*
> *presented as a prayerful consideration of one's*
> *past, but with a major focus on the future.*
> —Richard McBrien,
> *Encyclopedia of Catholicism*[1]

Day 38

How Far Will You Go?

September 3, 2013

Great crowds were traveling with Jesus,
and he turned and addressed them,
"If anyone comes to me without
hating his father and mother,
wife and children, brothers and sisters,
and even his own life,
he cannot be my disciple.
Whoever does not carry his own cross
and come after me cannot be my disciple.
    –Luke 14:26--33

ONCE LONG AGO, I sat in my office with a young couple I had married less than a year before. She was determined to end the marriage as quickly as possible. She had found married life not to her liking. Her friends were all single, going out and meeting interesting men, while she was stuck in a small apartment with her dull husband. He was tedious, and their life together was full of routine. She wanted out as soon as possible. He was devastated and eager to conform to whatever behavior would keep her in the home. He was teary throughout the conversation and made ineffectual promises to change his stay-at-home ways. Eventually, out of desperation, he got down on his hands and knees, grabbed her legs and begged her not to leave him. It was heartbreaking to witness and an unforgettable example of how far an individual was willing to go out of love.

The parish I serve has a tradition of celebrating its parish feast as a "Jubilee Sunday." We cancel all the masses except one and rent a great tent inviting all the parishioners to come to a single celebration followed by barbecues, raffles and games for the children. A planning committee studies the readings in advance and discerns a theme to explore. This Sunday's challenging gospel is partially presented to you at the top of the page, and from this we culled the question/theme *"how far will you go?"* Jesus clearly states how nothing is to stand before our relationship with God. All distractions must be eliminated. And so, this weekend we will consider the boundaries we are willing to cross in order to protect our spiritual lives.

It is such a compelling overall question, don't you think? How far are we willing to go for love, money, God, children, success, pleasure? History books are filled with stories of our ancestors crossing oceans and waging wars for freedom, for love, for God. Would we? Could we surrender a bodily organ so that another person might thrive? Would we be willing to give up a week's holiday to work in a developing country? Would you abandon your dignity and get down on the floor and beg someone you love not to leave you? How far would you go for something vital? Perhaps we will never know the answer to that question until the day comes and we are in danger of losing something precious.

DAY 39

That's Entertainment!

September 6, 2013

M Y MOTHER LOVES TO TALK ABOUT the Golden Age of Hollywood. She describes going into the movie theatres of her childhood and being swept away by Fred Astaire, Clark Gable, Judy Garland, and Esther Williams. Her theory: Those films made the viewer feel good. The music, dancing and wholesome love stories gave the audience hope and buoyancy. Throughout a lifetime of this repeated conversation, I found myself internally (*and all right, often externally*) rolling my eyes in an unwillingness to accept this viewpoint. I enjoyed gritty dramas and wry Woody Allen comedies. As a college student, I sat through midnight showings of the *Rocky Horror Picture Show* and *Godfather* marathons. I entered eagerly into discussions about the technique of Ingmar Bergman and subliminal messaging of David Lynch.

However, I am beginning to wonder if perhaps my mother was right all along?

I recently watched a violent movie on television about a group of young people caught up in a Mexican drug cartel. It was an exciting, well-made and I suspect a very accurate portrayal of that seamy world, but when the picture was over, I was exhausted and depressed. There was a time when I would have been intrigued by a glimpse into such a dangerous atmosphere; however, now I feel impatience with the foolishness of the characters' decisions and their horrific consequences. What has changed in me? Is it merely that I am getting older or has my taste naturally flipped? I have always gone to movies with a great interest in what was being made and how cinema reflected the consciousness of the times. I think I went into one movie theatre all summer long, and I hated the movie and could not wait to go home!

I remember there was a Dan Brown thriller being released several years ago, and while discussing its upcoming arrival with an elderly parishioner, she expressed surprise that anyone would want to subject themselves to such material, "Why would you want to put that into your head?" she questioned.

I must admit that when I see previews for horror films on television—flashes of chainsaws, blood and screaming teenagers, I must agree with my parishioner. Two hours of that and you would never get me out from underneath my bed! Perhaps it is because I am already bombarded with terrifying images of cruelty and injustice in the news that I find myself craving Julia Roberts in a romantic comedy or James Bond stylishly subduing the enemy in a perfectly cut tuxedo. For whatever reason, I need recreational material that makes me laugh, displays beauty and perhaps even gives me some crackling dialog to dwell upon as I drift off to sleep.

I hate to admit it, but my mother was right; if I am going to spend my time looking at something, I want it to raise me up . . . so I can do the same for you on Sunday.

DAY 40

 С3

Syria

September 10, 2013

I WONDER IF THERE WILL ALWAYS BE upheaval in the world. In spite of all we have learned about the consequences of cruelty and combat, here we are again. It's a terrible place to be—having to decide: what is the right thing to do? In these crucial moments, before commitments are made and actions put into motion, I remember a quote I saw in the Mahatma Gandhi exhibit last year in the Nobel Peace Museum in Oslo, Norway:

> *When I despair, I remember that all through*
> *history the ways of truth and love have always*
> *won. There have been tyrants and murderers, and*
> *for a time they can seem invincible, but in the end,*
> *they always fall. Think of it—always."*
> –Mahatma Gandhi

Day 41

One Beautiful Thing

September 13, 2013

The one who seeks beauty will find it.
–Bill Cunningham

JUST FINISHED A NOVEL I LOVED. Not a volume I hoped would be funnier, more insightful or deeper, but a wonderfully satisfying tale about an interesting character who possessed humorous insights and rich details to share about the adventure of life. I loved the book and hated for it to end. It taught me something about life I had not known, and it did not cause me to groan my way through some labyrinthine tome but provided insight through the most entertaining of mediums: a story!

The narrator of the tale is a middle-aged man living in New York City, disdainfully working for an advertising company. He is in love with his young assistant with whom he has playful interactions over the telephone. Between them, they have this "*bit*" they share in the midst of their daily communications: They call it, "one beautiful thing." Each day they would tell one another one beautiful thing they had seen or experienced. It was often something mundane or seemingly innocuous. However, knowing they must recount the one beautiful thing each day gave them a heightened sense of awareness in their surroundings and in the interactions of the people around them.

What a hopeful quest—each day to seek that one thing of beauty, courage, kindness or eloquence that lifts you. I suspect we are becoming increasingly blind to the search for beauty with our splintering attention spans and an unquenchable thirst for instant gratification. And yet, even in our busy and distracted world, there are examples of generosity, abundance and wonder.

With this action in mind, I was walking in the charming downtown district of the town where I live and noticed an elderly gentleman sitting contentedly in front of a small coffee shop. He was not poking at a hand-held technological device, he did not appear lonely, rather he was sitting with his legs propped up upon the empty chair in front of him with his face lifted up to the fall sunlight. When I glanced at him, he smiled at me in such a way as if to say, "Isn't this the life, sitting in the sun with a perfect cup of coffee." Observing such simple contentment is my one beautiful thing today.

I wonder if each of us were responsible for reporting the one beautiful thing we see or experience each day, if we would not find ourselves less pessimistic, less aggravated, more in love with the life we are given as an unpredictable present that opens in unexpected ways to test our endurance and ingenuity.

> *Who can know what goes on in someone else's life?*
> *In their worries and fears and hopes.*
> *Their history and pain.*
> *Who knows the quiet joy that one might feel in the*
> *quotidian thing,*
> *the nothing thing; a child's evening bath,*
> *volunteering at a soup kitchen,*
> *walking the dog when the family is asleep, the*
> *neighborhood quiet,*
> *a cigarette smoked alone.*
> *Lunch with a favorite coworker.*
> *Who can know the little worlds of beauty*
> *we try desperately to guard during the onslaught:*
> *watching your wife go through chemo;*
> *your father waste away from Alzheimer's;*
> *your sister relapse into alcoholism.*
> *The simple truth is that we know nothing*
> *about the inner life of the person sitting next to us on*
> *the plane, in the subway,*
> *the car behind us in traffic.*
> *We know nothing unless we choose to listen.*
> *Quiet desperation? What about quiet resilience.*
> *Quiet courage. Quiet hope.*
> >   –John Kenny, *Truth in Advertising*[1]

Day 42

After YOU!

September 17, 2013

ERE IN CALIFORNIA, we are almost always in a state of spaciousness. Even when stuck in a miserable traffic jam, we still have the boundary of the car surrounding us. However, when in New York City, humanity always seems to be squashed up against each other. You are always mashed into an elevator or squeezed into a theatre seat or jostled inside a mob attempting to view Van Gogh's *Starry Night*. Something about that world brings out the best in me. Perhaps it is because I do not live in that mad setting, I find it easier and more enjoyable to extend courtesy as I make my way through the city. I always make a point of saying "good morning" when I step into the elevator, holding the door open for the individual behind me, or making sure I am not stepping ahead of the person staring at the menu in a caffeine-deficient daze at Starbucks. I relish the look of surprise and pleasure when I extend these small gestures, and I feel an instant lift in my mood and disposition by offering some small courtesy to a stranger.

What a beautiful word: *courtesy*. Webster's definition: "marked by respect for and consideration of others." I would suggest that courtesy is at the foundation of Christianity. When considering the stories of Jesus and his interactions with others, don't you view him as consistently extending respect to those with whom he comes in contact? When he interacts with untouchables, dines with undesirables, forgives those deemed intolerable, he demonstrates consideration. Is it not Jesus who encourages us to let others go ahead to a higher place at the banquet table? Can you not see the miracle of turning water into wine as an effort to avoid embarrassment on behalf of the bridal party? Does he not avoid discourse that diminishes those who challenge and scorn him?

I find it discouraging how rude and abrupt we are becoming as a culture. Insensitivity and brusqueness all excused in homage to the god of convenience and expediency. It would appear to me that common courtesy is the grease that eases the rough edges of civilization. I suspect we may never know the impact some small act of kindness may have on the stranger but my hope is that when we make the effort to be patient and kind, when we notice someone struggling to get a stroller or walker through a doorway, when we take the time to offer a smile it might not only lighten another's burden but also create goodwill. Maybe courtesy is infectious. What if one act of courtesy is repaid by another and another until person by person, action by action, moment by moment, the world becomes a more gentle, loving and holy place?

> *Courtesy is the silver lining around the dark clouds*
> *of civilization;*
> *it is the best part of refinement,*
> *and in many ways, an art of heroic beauty*
> *in the vast gallery of man's cruelty and baseness.*
>> –Bryant H. McGill

DAY 43

❧

God and Money

September 20, 2013

EACH WEEK THE PREACHER FACES that horrible moment in which he or she must summon the idea upon which will become the foundation for the Sunday sermon. Even when the readings are dictated by the lectionary, even when the themes are clearly marked out, even when the preacher knows what must be said . . . there is a mountain range that must be scaled before that shining moment in which you open your mouth and speak with insight and wisdom. It occurs to me that there are manageable ways of communicating theological ideas about sexuality, forgiveness and even fortitude in the midst of adversity. However, the most difficult concept of all is money. This Sunday's gospel is ultimately about the battle that takes place between God and money.

How does one speak of this sensitive issue without alienating the congregation, or worse, bore them with so many biblical facts and details they simply mentally check out of the church building altogether? Is it possible to have a homiletic conversation that causes the listener to consider a spiritual perspective on finances? The rock-bottom truth is we need money. We need funding for medicine, nourishment, shelter, diversion and the mother lode— security. What a seductive idea *that* is. As if we could ever be safe and secure from danger, sickness or loneliness. Where is that place? Does it exist on this planet? Where is the exact location where all our fears are eliminated and we live in a state of perfect serenity? I believe Jesus is continually communicating that our only security is in God. It is not possible to love both the bankbook and the Creator. They are both jealous and require our undivided attention.

So if we need money and the maintenance of one's finances require attention, how do we find perspective? Perhaps the answer is to be found in asking the question: "What does money mean to me?"

I remember a quote by May Sarton in one of her journals in which she states that money translates for her into books, flowers, as well as the ability to create beauty and provide for an environment where loving others becomes possible. Something about her quote opened a door for me, and I agree that money is a means to an end, and if the end involves loving God, helping my neighbor or a stranger, and somehow making the world a more beautiful, safer, more abundant place for everyone then . . . so be it. I can sleep peacefully because what is really holding us together is not our net worth but the summation of our experiences and our willingness to overcome our wounds and self-pity so that we can convert our energy into loving God, one another, and ourselves.

> *That same night, I wrote my first short story.*
> *It took me thirty minutes.*
> *It was a dark little tale about a man who found a*
> *magic cup*
> *and learned that if he wept into the cup,*
> *his tears turned into pearls.*
> *But even though he had always been poor,*
> *he was a happy man and rarely shed a tear.*
> *So he found ways to make himself sad so that his*
> *tears could make him rich.*
> *As the pearls piled up, so did his greed grow.*
> *The story ended with the man sitting on a*
> *mountain of pearls,*
> *Knife in hand, weeping helplessly into the cup*
> *with his beloved wife's slain body in his arms.*
> –Khaled Hosseini, *The Kite Runner*[1]

Day 44

Excuse Me, Could You Say
That Again?

September 24, 2013

HAVE YOU EVER HAD A CONVERSATION where you expected the
other person to say something specific and they surprised
you? Honestly, most verbal exchanges have a predictable pattern
to them: weather, sports, achievements of children and health
concerns circle around the goal of appropriate repartee. I have
spent a lifetime dancing to the tedious steps of acceptable
topics of communication. And my entire professional life has
been dedicated to finding non-threatening ways of interpreting
the radical teachings of Jesus. Teachings that got him killed for
their inflammatory content. I only began to enjoy preaching once
I found my authentic way of speaking, but always feel confined
by the need to ease into the potentially churning waters of
controversy.

I am personally delighted to listen to someone who has a fresh, contemporary way of looking at the Jesus story. After years of listening to rather alienating papal commentary, it is taking me by surprise to hear the comments of Pope Francis, who in a recent interview said, *"We have to find a new balance, otherwise even the moral edifice of the Church is likely to fall like a house of cards, losing the freshness and fragrance of the Gospel."*

EXCUSE ME?

I beg your pardon?

Just when you think everything is inextricably mired in predictability, someone comes along and says something that takes your breath away. And make no mistake: he is beginning an entirely new conversation. And isn't that the way of the true prophet? Anyone can reheat old ideas and rant on familiar platforms. It is the authentic visionary who rises up and dares to reinterpret. Although, perhaps Pope Francis is actually borrowing old ideas himself; after all, when he states that the church should be a *"home for all,"* doesn't that sound a little like someone else? Who is it? Who was it that kept harping about loving our enemy and reaching out to the poor; who was it that embraced and welcomed the outcasts of society? Hmmm . . . oh, I can't remember! Can you?

DAY 45

Balance After a Fall

September 27, 2013

WHEN YOU WATCH THE OLYMPICS, there are athletes who balance on a narrow beam of wood. I suppose I consider all gymnasts to be superhuman, but for some reason, I always marvel at those girls finding equilibrium on the thinnest of surfaces. While I have no specific knowledge about any sporting competition, I suspect they are attempting to stabilize their body throughout the routine. When they turn, spin and jump they are constantly monitoring their weight and something as simple as a turn of the wrist, the angle of the neck and exact placement of the hip make the difference between finding balance and falling into disgrace.

I have felt a bit off center these last few months since the death of my father. I get confused about his absence and feel uncontrollably emotional. I almost selected a Father's Day card in June. And I find myself preparing to tell him things I think will amuse and entertain him. I don't believe there was anything specific left unsaid, but I suppose I just miss him and wonder . . . all the things people wonder when grieving excruciating loss. My spiritual director recently acknowledged the significance of this death by expressing the thought that our parents are "constellations in the universe of our lives. They are fixed and reliable, like a star that identifies our location."

Perhaps when a parent dies, we lose our bearings—something shifts in our own personal galaxy and we feel like we are falling off the beam. I suspect the aftermath of a death is a time in one's life of lost balance, but if I just remember the lessons my father taught me and apply those teachings slowly, carefully. If I monitor subtle movements of emotion and the specific distribution of tears, memory and laughter, I might find myself back on top. Moving through the world like the gymnast who leaps off a narrow strip of wood and lands perfectly on the surface of the earth.

> *You will weep and mourn while the*
> *world rejoices.*
> *You will grieve for a time*
> *but your grief will be turned into joy.*
> *When a woman is in labor,*
> *she is sad that her time has come.*
> *When she has borne her child,*
> *she no longer remembers her pain*
> *for joy that a human being has been born*

into the world.
In the same way, you are sad for a time,
but I shall see you again
and then your hearts will rejoice
will a joy no one can take from you.
>   –John 16:20-22

DAY 46

Building Bridges with Shaky Materials

October 1, 2013

Do one thing every day that scares you.
—Eleanor Roosevelt

I COULD NOT GET INTO THE BOOK. However, I loved the movie. This weekend I watched Ang Lee's brilliant adaptation of Yann Martel's book, *Life of Pi*. It was everything I love in a film: it took me to a faraway place, it had a twist in the end and it presented the world as a mystical place where God and nature can take the human person on an amazing journey. Pi is a young Indian boy whose family owns and operates a zoo. They are transporting the animals across the Pacific Ocean when the ship flounders in a storm. The young man finds himself alone on a lifeboat with a Bengal tiger. Pi is afraid of the beast but will not destroy him for fear of being completely alone in the middle of the vast and treacherous ocean. This preposterous circumstance is fraught with danger for Pi, but at one stage in the story, he acknowledges his fear of the tiger is good for it keeps him alert as the boat drifts endlessly across the sea.

I keep thinking about this idea that fear may have value. We are always trying to rid ourselves of apprehension and stress. I for one am always preaching the consistent directive from Jesus to "be not afraid." But what if fear has some value? Is dread not at the root of our inclination to stay away from dangerous hallucinatory drugs? Fright of being pulled over by law enforcement motivates us to drive automobiles safely. Distress at the prospect of displeasing God can inspire us to avoid sinful actions. Don't misunderstand me; I am not advocating a spirituality or even a lifestyle rooted in anxiety, rather if fear is inevitable, why not use it to our advantage?

When we sense the familiar inclination to worry about our money, health, family, I wonder if it is possible to allow the energy of fright to heighten our senses, engage our ingenuity, and activate creative solutions. In the same way that a person summons superhuman powers in an emergency, could our fear be a bridge to a solution? I suppose I am suggesting we make friends with the entirety of our personalities. Rather than running, denying or hiding—to accept that anxiety is a natural part of our survival. Perhaps we are meant to learn that healthy fear might be the very thing that saves us—like being with a tiger in a lifeboat waiting to be saved.

Bran thought about it. "Can a man still be brave if he's afraid?"

'That is the only time a man can be brave,' his father told him."

> –George R. R. Martin,
> *A Game of Thrones*

Day 47

Messengers and Guardians

October 4, 2013

DID YOU EVER SEE THAT MOVIE *City of Angels*? I loved it. Celestial beings roam the earth in packs attempting to offer protection to the human family. Nicholas Cage plays an angel who falls in love with a mortal woman, and he wants to convert into a living person in order to be with her. It's a fascinating story with a rather sad twist in the end. I was reminded of the film this week as the Church celebrated the Memorial of the Holy Guardian Angels. The Deacon in my parish preached the daily homily and talked about the biblical notion of angels. My mind went directly to the idea of various friends and strangers who were like angels to me in times of distress. But *his* homily encouraged the listener to consider the notion of God's messengers and how they function.

Richard McBrien, in his excellent *Encyclopedia of Catholicism*,[1] describes angels as:

> Supernatural beings who act as messengers of God. Contrary to artistic convention depicting them as winged, angels are represented in the Bible in the guise of human beings. They are sent to announce the birth of a child and its future destiny; they intercede before God and intervene in human affairs sometimes to protect, sometimes to execute judgment. It seems logical that God would create intermediaries who guide, communicate and protect. After all, everyone needs assistance as we attempt to cope with the unpredictability of life.

It is comforting to consider the possibility of a spirit with you on the freeway, in the waiting room at the hospital and right beside your child on the first day of school. I have certainly been the recipient of some very kind and generous people, but it's reassuring to think that just beyond the curve of your eye is God's messenger—waiting for that moment to stop the car, guide the hand of the surgeon or break your fall and save you.

GUARDIAN ANGEL PRAYER
Angel of God,
my guardian dear,
to whom God's love commits me here,
ever this day or night be at my side,
to light and guard,
to rule and guide. Amen.

Day 48

Living in a Nightmare

October 11, 2013

> *Do not spoil what you have by desiring what you*
> *have not; remember that what you now have was*
> *once among the things you only hoped for.*
> –Epicurus

I AM ACQUAINTED WITH A MIDDLE-AGED COUPLE who would appear from the outside to be living the dream. They have a lovely, comfortable home, nice well-equipped cars, healthy, grown children and take frequent excursions to pleasant nearby getaway destinations. And yet, they seem fundamentally unhappy with their lot in life. The usual greeting of "*how are you'*" is responded to with a sigh and a look of world-weariness. When you question their response, they specify the standard Sturm and Drang that is part of every life. As I repeatedly listen to their litany of dissatisfaction, I tend to consider the multitude of individuals who would joyfully change places with this couple.

I often remind my parishioners that we are marketed into a state of restlessness by the economic engine that drives our economy. It's elementary, my dear Watson—if I manufacture automobiles and can convince you that your current transportation is shabby and outdated, then the next phase of my master plan persuades that a new purchase will make you slimmer, attractive to younger men and women, and your entire life will be filled with admiration, sunshine and sexual magnetism. I understand this marketing technique and have even been seduced by its brilliant ability to creep inside my brain and uncover my hidden longings. However, the sinister underbelly of this relentless performance means that we are never happy. *"If only . . ."* we tell ourselves. *"If only I had that car, that house, that credential. If only I had those abs and that country house, that financial bonus, then I would finally and forever be happy."*

It's like a curse from a childhood fairytale—to be in perpetual dissatisfaction with what one possesses. In the stories from our childhood, it's always some wicked creature that casts a spell and the entire tale is a search for a solution. Well, I think I have it: not true love's kiss, (*that never hurts by the way*) not magic-jeweled shoes, nor an incantation by a professor from Hogwarts. The antidote from self-pity, greed and discontent is gratitude.

This Sunday's readings are about the power of appreciation. When the ugly monster of disappointment surfaces on your consciousness, you can trap and tame it by merely considering the infinite blessings of your existence. Clean water, a hot shower, friends who make you laugh, a great book, lemon-meringue pie, your grandmother's china, cheeseburgers with fries, Clark Gable in *Gone With the Wind,* and Julia Roberts in *Pretty Woman,* nature, the smell of the rain, the song from your first dance and the words of Jesus who told us we are loved by God. Jesus, who shows us that anything is possible—even life after death. The next time you feel the presence of the Gorgon of displeasure, just summon those images of thankfulness. Replay them in your mind like a slideshow. The beast despises contentment—face the monster with satisfaction and the monster simply disappears.

> *Piglet noticed that even though he had a Very*
> *Small Heart, it could hold a rather large amount of*
> *Gratitude.*
> —A. A. Milne, *Winnie-the-Pooh*

DAY 49

"Going Up?"

October 15, 2013

*God is the light that illuminates the darkness, even
if it does not dissolve it,
and a spark of divine light is within each of us. In a
letter I wrote to you,
you will remember I said that our species will end
but the light of God will not end and at that point,
it will invade all souls and it will be in everyone....
Transcendence remains because that light, all
in everything, transcends the universe and the
species it inhabits at that stage.*

—Pope Francis

I LOVE THAT WORD *transcendence*. Webster's defines transcend as: "the ability to rise above or extend notably beyond ordinary limits." I often wonder, is it possible for us to rise above our normal limits? I see people who appear to ascend above and beyond the snags and bumps that hold me prisoner. I observe with great envy individuals who seem to move through life with their feet just slightly above the ground. How do they do it? How does one step up and over the slick, dark patches of betrayal and disappointment? What operating system are they on? And more importantly, where do I download?

The above quote from our new and quite dazzling Pope would suggest that there is something greater inside the human person enabling us to link with a superior strength, courage and wisdom than we personally possess. My Spiritual Director is always (*irritatingly*) reminding me to discuss my anxieties with God in prayer. He wants me to ask God why my mind replays the past and dwells in places of regret. Perhaps I am reluctant to open this dialog for fear that God might actually release me from familiar preoccupations and lift me skyward? Maybe we human beings are always just a little nervous about heights.

I suppose there is an extraordinary distinction to be made between the person who stands on the curb and marvels at the altitude of a tower and the other personality who immediately (*or eventually, in my case*) decides to climb to the top and take in the great vista. It must be a tremendous view from the skyscraper of freedom, forgiveness, hope and infinite possibilities. I don't think I can manage the express elevator but I am prepared to take the stairs . . . even if it takes a lifetime.

Day 50

Thank You

October 18, 2013

> *Jesus told his disciples a parable*
> *about the necessity for them to pray*
> *always without becoming weary.*
> –Luke 18:1

I JUST SAW THE NEW MOVIE *Gravity* in 3D! And I am still vibrating! Sandra Bullock plays an astronaut on a space station performing some routine repair tasks when debris smashes into the vessel and casts her adrift into space. And when I use the word "smash," I mean it. Wearing the 3D glasses made me feel as if I were in the collision myself. Splintering fragments of wreckage seemingly zooming toward my face had me weaving and bobbing in my seat. One frantic moment has the main character attempting to survive yet another in a series of catastrophes and muttering the statement that no one ever taught her how to pray. Toward the end of the film, after having survived innumerable mishaps and near death, she glances up to the sky and says the words, "*thank you.*" It's a beautiful moment reminding me of a quote by Meister Eckhart, who wrote, "*If the only prayer you said was thank you, that would be enough.*"

This Sunday Jesus tells a parable about a persistent widow who is unrelenting in her desire for a just legal decision from an indifferent judge. The application of the parable is to be found in understanding how tenacity in prayer will be rewarded. However, I cannot help but wonder if Eckhart is not alluding to another layer of depth in his statement. What if the greatest prayer is gratitude? If God knows our needs better than we ourselves and if our life experiences have the potential of enhancing our awareness, what if "thank you" offered consistently in prayer is the key that unlocks the doorway to understanding?

It's a tall order—untiring gratitude—to be thankful for the entire journey, even those elements we dread. Is it possible that we are meant to understand that everything that happens has the potential of broadening our compassion and our understanding? What if the most humbling circumstance enables us to finally become generous, tolerant or kind? If in the midst of disease, bankruptcy or some other horror we finally encounter the living God—is that not a reason to be appreciative? And when words seem inadequate to express the enormity of our feelings, just say *thank you*—that would appear to sum it all up.

Cultivate the habit of being grateful for everything that comes to you, and to give thanks continuously. And because all things have contributed to your advancement, you should include all things in your gratitude.

–Ralph Waldo Emerson

Day 51

One. Single. Person.

October 24, 2013

In conclusion, just as through one transgression
Condemnation came upon all,
So, through one righteous act
Acquittal and life came to all.
For just as through the disobedience of one man
the many were made sinners,
so, through the obedience of one
the many will be made righteous.
　　　　–Paul to the Church at Rome
　　　　Romans 5:18-19

M ANY YEARS AGO, I was proclaiming the gospel at a Sunday
morning mass, when an elderly woman became non-

responsive. Her adult daughter began screaming. It was a small church filled to capacity, and it took a while to calm the young woman and address the situation. I learned a valuable lesson that day: It only takes one person to create a panic. Actually, it only takes one person to have an idea that eventually becomes Apple Computer, Google, a symphony, a war, a theology, or the cure to a disease. Consider for a moment the amazing power of one single person.

Most of us go through life feeling power-*less*. It is natural to feel like a useless cog when stuck in a relentless traffic jam, or battling some bureaucracy, or flummoxed by some unsolvable family dilemma. President Obama, Jeff Bezos, Steven Spielberg are powerful. By contrast, I am small, insignificant and beleaguered. This week while preaching at the daily mass on the above reading from Saint Paul, I found myself fascinated by the enormity of his proposal. Paul is stating that at a moment in history, there was a disconnect between one individual and God, and that crack began an aftershock of cosmic division. One person began this destruction and through yet another single person harmony was restored between the human family and the Creator. What he is actually describing is the extraordinary power each human person has for good and for destruction.

I wonder how different our culture would be if we all considered the fantastic significance we bring to our world. How would our communities be altered if we displayed a consistent countenance of encouragement, acceptance and inclusion? What would be the shape of each new day if we believed ourselves capable of strength, wisdom and ingenuity? Saint Paul states that a single person made a universal mess and another one cleaned it up! And the Son of God describes us as made in the image and likeness of the greatest force of positive energy in the cosmos.

If we could just believe that each day brings refreshed opportunity to improve the atmosphere of the planet, then maybe, finally, the world might just become a more peaceful, more loving, more holy place.

Day 52

It's Awfully Noisy Down Here!

October 29, 2013

In today's gig economy, where jobs have been replaced by "portfolios of projects," most people find themselves doing more things less well for two-thirds of the money. The—we—text each other we're "crazed." Then comes a frenzy of activity accomplishing nothing much. Much of the working day is spent papering over a job half done from the day before. Voicemails vanish into the void. Messages from colleagues, to say nothing of friends, are buried forever under the email avalanche. Everywhere you turn, people feel stranded by holes in the chain of command. No one has time, in all the hyper-connectivity, to talk about the details, the structure, the unglamorous granularity of how things get done.

–Tina Brown, *The Daily Beast* [1]

T HE OTHER MORNING, after daily mass, a parishioner meekly asked if she might have a word with me. As I willingly led her to my office, I was struck by the luxury of being able to accept her last-minute request. In my former parish, I would have looked at such a person with disbelief. I had engagements booked up weeks ahead of time. My daily schedule was crammed with office appointments, funerals, meetings, schedules, and visits to hospitals, classrooms, nursing homes and staff meetings. If a parishioner (*or an innocent bystander*) had asked me for an impromptu meeting, I might have detonated!

I often consider how frantic our world has become. Tina Brown, in her editorial quoted at the top of the page, captures for me the frenetic atmosphere we live in. The feeling of dread when we open our email and find an endless spool of messages and communiqués. The mechanical voice mail server who announces that you have twenty-four messages. The blur of faces on a Sunday when one has five or six liturgies. It's no wonder people have road rage or surrender to substance abuse. We are worn out and overstimulated—even "*relaxing*" in front of the television is to subject yourself to a barrage of images, noise, and marketing.

Is it me or do you sense a shift away from all this racket? Am I being idealistic or is the paradigm swinging toward a simpler, quieter, easier life? Most of my friends want a smaller house than the one they are currently living in. They are uncluttering their attics, closets and drawers. The greed and materialism seem to be abating, and a desire for peace, simplicity and the extravagance of viewing nature, listening to your loved ones and the bliss of silence are becoming the goals of my generation. Perhaps this is why Jesus cautioned his disciples to live without multiple belongings and Thoreau suggested "simplicity." Maybe the greatest indulgence we can acquire is to cultivate an atmosphere in which we are able to listen to a request and instead of screaming, calmly say "yes."

> Our life is frittered away by detail. An honest man
> has hardly need to count more than his ten fingers,
> or in extreme cases he may add his ten toes, and
> lump the rest. Simplicity, simplicity, simplicity! I
> say, let your affairs be as two or three, and not a
> hundred or a thousand; instead of a million count
> half a dozen, and keep your accounts on your
> thumbnail. In the midst of this chopping sea of
> civilized life, such are the clouds and storms and
> quicksands and thousand-and-one items to be
> allowed for, that a man has to live, if he would not
> founder . . .
> –Henry David Thoreau

Day 53

Just Make It Go Away!

November 5, 2013

A FRIEND OF MINE told me a story last week about her former employer who was a high-powered real estate developer. When in the midst of some professional snarl, he would instruct his assistant to *"just make it all go away!"* What a glorious idea: in the midst of life's messes could there be someone who would make a few phone calls, deliver some pay-offs, hire an assassin and . . . ***poof!*** All unsolvable problems vanish? "Just make it all go away" is the ultimate luxury. Is that not what we tell our physicians and surgeons, our tax accountants and mechanics? Is this not the dream and expectation of every life—that all unpleasantness is to be banished from the freeway of our lives so we can zoom into even greater stratospheres of efficiency, pleasure and fulfillment?

I could not help but wonder if we don't incorporate this

same idea into our prayer lives as well. How often have I told God to make my suffering go away? I cannot recount the number of prayers dictating storylines to the Creator of the Universe. I believe I am beginning to enter into a new awareness in which I am eager not to escape or attract unpleasant circumstances, but rather to understand and decode the entirety of my life's experiences.

If I told you a story free from conflict or effort would you be entertained? I suspect not. What makes any story compelling is the overcoming of obstacles, the acquisition of wisdom, the realization of unknown strength and courage. If your existence is actually the story of your life, should it not be filled with the full spectrum of emotion and experience? And doesn't that include heartbreak, failure and rejection as well as triumph and success? To wish away the challenges of life would leave us with what? Plateau after plateau? I'll await that never-ending vista in heaven.

For now, I pray for good humor as I search for meaning; I pray for perseverance in cultivating love; and I pray for a great, passionate, unforgettable story starring my God, my neighbor and myself!

DAY 54

"Coulda, Woulda, Shoulda"

November 9, 2013

RECENTLY A FRIEND OF MINE was recounting the details of an ancient love affair. The discussion included descriptions of their time together, the acceleration of discontent and an explosive separation. However, the main theme of the discourse seemed to be the lingering question of would she have been happier with *HIM*. Would she be more fulfilled; would she live in a better house; who would her friends be, and what clothes would she be wearing in that alternate universe? In that world, undoubtedly, everything would be preferable to the selections she actually made. That decor would be perfect, that husband attentive, and everything would be brighter, tastier and more organized. Whenever I am bored, lonely or clogged in some tedious task, my mind immediately reverts to that familiar song;

like clicking my iPod to repeat my favorite track . . . *what if I had chosen a different path?*

I am convinced this is a bewitching mind trap—looking back at decisions made in the past and questioning our choices. Twenty-five years ago I surrendered to a full-blown anxiety attack and began to dismantle all my ordination plans. Approximately a month before becoming a priest, I woke up with the absolute certainty that I was about to make a crushing mistake. On that hellish day, all my painstaking vocational discernment shattered around me and escape became the most reasonable option I could devise. Like a passenger on a floundering ship forced to choose what should be taken and what left behind, I imagined myself walking away from my future life as a priest and constructing something ultimately preferable. Fortunately cooler heads prevailed and talked me off the ledge. What remains from that grim day was a friend who counseled me to stop, breathe and remember what decisions had been made when I was calm and without the stress of an imminent major commitment.

That wise counsel has been a gift I reuse over and over in my life: the belief that rational, prayerful decisions are to be trusted. Considering the specific information we possess, our state of mind and the circumstances surrounding us, we need to have faith we make prudent life choices that reflect who we are meant to be. Who wants to live with regret, or worse, waste what little time we have wondering what might have been?

Looking back at the scrapbook of our lives can be enjoyable, but when it sours into anguish, bitterness and disappointment it's time to go get a frozen yogurt . . . *with sprinkles!* And while you're enjoying that treat, stop, take a breath and remember that every decision you have made has brought you to this perfect moment. A moment filled with imperfections, wrong turns, friends, memories, heartache, happenstance, mystery, moonlight, football games, music and love. Summarize all those experiences and choices, then go look at yourself in the mirror and see who you really are.

> But Jesus said to him, "No one, having put his hand to the plow, and looking back, is fit for the kingdom of God."
> –Luke 9:62

Day 55

Learning a Lesson at
the Symphony

November 16, 2013

M Y MOTHER NOW LIVES in a midwestern town near my brother and his wife, who are musicians. On a recent visit, I attended a symphony concert in which they were performing. In our ultra-technological world, this activity seemed like such a deliciously old-fashioned thing to do. Something about getting dressed up to *watch* people make music made me feel like a character from Henry James or Edith Wharton. It was splendid. Sitting in the auditorium while strings, woodwinds, and percussion combined to fill the space with Strauss and Tchaikovsky was remarkably refreshing. The movement of the conductor fascinated me—how delicate and massive gestures were matched by the musicians. I surrendered to the passion and drama of the music. For a time, I was not checking my phone, preparing a homily or making a mental *to-do list*; I was merely sitting and listening with complete absorption while sound and energy blasted through me.

I cannot help but wonder if that world is disappearing. Will future generations be interested in funding such endeavors? Obviously, it costs dearly to pay for a symphony orchestra, a public library, a theatre company. If I let myself, I could begin to panic at the thought of the vanishing arts and sciences. And yet, they still exist. Performances continue to be sponsored by generous donors, students are still attempting to master the cello, and Shakespeare's soliloquies are committed to memory. When I make the effort, I can see there is still a world out there of music, drama and poetry if one is willing to participate.

Why all this anxiety about the arts? Because in spite of how much I love technology (*and believe me, I love it*) technology can never replace the importance of people gathering to listen in silence to beautiful music or laugh together at the wit of Neil Simon. The same dynamic camaraderie that happens at a ball game occurs when we focus our collective attention on the arts. The inherent danger of technology is the isolation it encourages: the encroaching sensibility that we need not leave our cocoon of immediate gratification.

Would I have gone to the symphony if my family was not performing? Probably not. It might be boring; there will be inconveniences; I'm tired. The excuses become a mountain too arduous to scale. However, when we rouse ourselves and go to the concert, see the play, attend the reading, there is balm for the soul that is starving from malnutrition. When we go, when we see, when we listen, something happens inside that cannot be defined in words: we are changed; we are warmed . . . the beauty of the human journey can be revealed.

Day 56

Courage

November 22, 2013

I HAVE A PARISHIONER who has been diagnosed with a grave illness. It will most likely require some dreadful upcoming treatment. In our conversations, I have found her practical and good-humored. I have such admiration for the person who holds onto the ability to laugh in the face of adversity. I suspect that life has a way of wearing away at the ability to find mirth in the face of disappointment and heartbreak. Often I meet people whose circumstances have blasted every last belly laugh into smithereens. These are usually the same individuals who, upon overhearing hilarity, tend to ask in a querulous tone of voice, "What's so funny?"

This is not intended to be a reflection on humor so much as a glimpse into courage. I would suggest one definition of this word being the ability to face adversity without self-pity. The fact is that everyone, yes everyone, has some kind of challenge, misfortune or dilemma they are attempting to overcome. We are all trying to scale the wall of the past, eradicate a cancer cell, or pay off a crippling debt. Even the goon at the next restaurant table with the annoyingly braying laugh (*that man is probably me by the way*) is probably attempting to hold his fraying marriage together. Just because we are laughing or telling a funny story does not mean we don't experience suffering—it usually means we are hoping to transcend it.

Ernest Hemingway wrote, *Courage is grace under pressure.* For me, that grace is exhibited when in the face of crisis we still find the ability to say "good morning" and "thank you." When we continue to ask the polite question and are willing to patiently listen to a long and pointless story. Whining and self-absorption can be diverting but after a while, they leave a sour taste in one's mouth. I hope that nothing is so beastly that I cannot appreciate the beauty in the colors of the sky or savor my favorite music or laugh out loud at my own behavior. After all, this is my one and only trip—I would like to enjoy the ride.

> *Courage is not the absence of fear, but rather the judgment that something else is more important than fear.*
> –Ambrose Redmoon

Day 57

Midnight Confession

December 10, 2013

MY FATHER HAD THE GIFT.

A man I work with has it. And sometimes I wonder if they realize how fortunate they are? The remarkable ability to put one's head down on a pillow and drift into a refreshing sleep. Everything I read today emphasizes the need for slumber. Physicians describe how we are sleep deprived, and this lack is prematurely aging us, causing us to make mistakes at work, and be short-tempered with our families and colleagues. I agree with these experts—and I experience the benefits when I have good rest and the physical limitations when ensnared by insomnia. And I would go so far as to claim that I have read a good number of books and articles offering tips and solutions for those of us who lay awake at night tossing and fretting. These "tips" include drinking warm water throughout the day, eating only certain foods, restricting oneself to a rigid schedule of rising and getting into bed. These "Sleep Sages" recommend all organic sheeting, lavender candles and calcium tablets.

Truthfully, I have adopted some of these practices and sometimes experience the advantages of this collective wisdom and often not. It can be terrifying to awaken in the middle of the night with the realization that a full and demanding day awaits—a day in which one needs a full night of rest in order to function with equilibrium. We know that in that moment turning on the television, activating the iPad, reaching for the library book is deadly. These distractions will only enhance alertness. So why not have a nocturnal conversation with God? Use this quiet, sacred time as a moment to engage the Holy? Rather than surrender to panic and fear, turn your attention to the God of our lives who waits for any opportunity to engage us.

Honestly, in that moment we are at our most vulnerable—the usual psychological and emotional shields are down. It is an advantageous time to speak the truth of who we really are and what we really need. It's in those quiet, focused moments that it becomes possible to hear that soft, whispering sound of God's voice. Just take a breath. Gaze into the darkness and refocus your attention upon the resonate presence of the Creator. Tell God what has awakened you, what haunts you; describe the specifics of your deepest desire. Keep monitoring your breath and relax into the knowledge that you are loved and you are not alone—not even in the middle of the night.

A strong and heavy wind
was rending the mountains
and crushing rocks
before the Lord—but the Lord was not in the
wind.
After the wind there was
an earthquake—but the Lord was not in the
earthquake.
After the earthquake
there was a fire—but the Lord was not in the fire.
After the fire there was a tiny whispering sound.
When he heard this,
Elijah hid his face in his cloak
and went and stood at the entrance of the cave.

      –The Book of Kings (1 Kings 19:11)

I've always envied people who sleep easily.
Their brains must be cleaner,
the floorboards of the skull well swept,
all the little monsters closed up
in a steamer trunk at the foot of the bed.

      –David Benioff, *City of Thieves*

Day 58

"Bah Humbug"

December 17, 2013

I CANNOT PUT MY FINGER ON exactly when I lost my Christmas spirit. I have such wonderful memories of my childhood Christmases. We always went to Midnight Mass and so Christmas day was entirely dedicated to presents and a feast. There were newly acquired toys, games and books to read. A fully stoked fireplace would be burning all day and there would be naps taken by everyone after such a late night and early morning. I suppose all people eventually surrender the effortless unfolding of that day as we move into adulthood. If we have a family we are now engineering that experience for them. For myself, I went from enjoying that perfect day prepared by my parents to priesthood where I felt responsible for the church component of Christmas for hundreds of people. Without being too specific the obligations of the season feel like an avalanche of details and drudgery. With the passing of every December day, I feel the list grow longer and my spirit sagging into inertia and weariness.

For many years I worked with a woman completely unsympathetic to my self-pity. In her perspective, it was my responsibility as a pastor to lift up my parishioners and assist in the merriment of the season. She "*suggested*" that no one was interested in yet another complaining personality. Christmas and Advent are a time for great rejoicing in the lives of people who are struggling to stay afloat so in essence **"buck up and get to work."** At the time I felt she was horribly insensitive but now, many years later, I see her unpleasant point. Feeling sorry for myself feels like such a selfish occupation when I have so many blessings I could never count them all.

Why should one go around with a gloomy façade simply because one is busy and tired? The fact is everyone is busy and tired. Everyone is overextended and anxious and maybe the best way we can prepare to celebrate the feast of Christmas is by offering good cheer. To offer up prayers full of gratitude and hope can distract us from all the troubling or worrisome details of our lives. There is so much to celebrate and rejoicing seems like the least we can do in the face of so many blessings and opportunities. So why not join me (*however reluctantly*) this Advent and Christmas by being gentle with one another, listening carefully when someone speaks, offering the other motorist a chance to enter into our lane of traffic. Let's be grateful and send out a shout of elation in the midst of this incredibly busy time because we are the children of God and all things are possible—even joy!

Rejoice in the Lord always! I say it again. Rejoice!
Everyone should see how unselfish you are.
The Lord is near. Dismiss all anxiety from your
minds. Present your needs to God in every form
of gratitude. Then God's own peace, which is
beyond all understanding, will stand guard over
your hearts and minds, in Christ Jesus. Finally, your
thoughts should be wholly directed to all that is
true, all that deserves respect, all that is honest,
pure, admirable, decent, virtuous, or worthy of
praise. Live according to what you have learned
and accepted, what you have heard me say and
seen me do. Then will the God of peace be with
you.

–Philippians 4:4–9

DAY 59

∝

A Christmas Card from the Country Priest

December 24, 2013

L AST WEEK I MADE A QUICK TRIP to deliver out-of-town gifts and made a brief stop at the home of a friend who loves her home. I blasted in from the freeway and walked into a Christmas sanctuary. My friend's home was perfectly decorated with glowing trees and fragrant holiday candles. She was adorned with an apron and the electric mixer was actually whirring with batter and cookie sheets were positioned on the countertop awaiting the concoction. The kitchen smelled of vanilla, cinnamon and most intoxicating of all—chocolate. It was such a perfect world. I could imagine even Martha Stewart giving the environment her grudging nod of approval! And while it was not my home or perhaps will never be the world I inhabit, it lifted my spirit.

For a person who has difficulty entering into the joyful nature of Christmas, I am amazed how certain small elements have the ability to elevate my leaden disposition. Reading Christmas cards from old friends, seeing the delight on the faces of people who are the recipients of presents, going to a sing-along holiday concert have provided me with a refreshing sense of what Christmas can be. I cannot help but wonder if sometimes we are just in the habit of feeling stressed or overwhelmed and simply cannot see the opportunities for surprise, delight and enjoyment.

So be good to yourselves this Christmas holiday season. Take a nap, read a mystery, get in the car and drive down a street decorated with lights. Walk into your church and send up a prayer of gratitude for the adventure of your life. Pay a compliment to the department store clerk as you return your Christmas gifts—it is amazing how those little gestures make a difference, cheer us up and make everything, *everything* better!

Happiness at Christmastime!

The angel said to them: "You have nothing
to fear! I come to proclaim good news to you—
tidings of great joy to be shared by the
whole people.
This day in David's city a savior has been born to
you, the Messiah and Lord."
    –Luke 2:10–14

Day 60

White/Write Out

February 24, 2014

WHERE WAS I? What was I saying? You know, before I was so rudely interrupted . . . by a **BLIZZARD!**

That's right sisters and brothers; the Country Priest drove a car through a blizzard in the Dakotas! I have never been near a blizzard or given thought to what such a phenomenon might be like. Well, it's like this: you are driving a vehicle into blowing snow and suddenly the snowstorm becomes a blanket that covers the entire world. You no longer have a sense of the distinction between the earth and sky. Everything is silent, white and deadly. And it is unclear where you are or how to navigate. You've lost your bearings and wonder if you will ever return to a safe place? Life sometimes feels like a blizzard of storms and confusions—deaths and rebirths. We feel lost and then miraculously found:

threatened and then safe.

After Christmas, I stopped writing in my *Journal of a Country Priest*. Originally it was because I was traveling, preoccupied, taking care of my mother and driving into blizzards. And then one week becomes another, and as the days flashed by, I found myself questioning the reason for the journal and became blinded by the possibility of its irrelevance. What is my purpose? And what do God and the reader desire? These compelling questions are unanswered, but I suspect revelation is not to be found in unproductive pondering but in writing, telling stories and asking questions, as I strain my ear to hear the tiny whispering sound of God's voice as I drive through the storm.

> *A strong and heavy wind was rending the*
> *mountains and crushing rocks before the Lord—*
> *but the Lord was not in the wind.*
> *After the wind there was an earthquake—but the*
> *Lord was not in the earthquake.*
> *After the earthquake there was a fire—but the*
> *Lord was not in the fire.*
> *After the fire there was a tiny whispering sound.*
> *When he heard this,*
> *Elijah hid his face in his cloak and went and stood*
> *at the entrance of the cave.*
> 　　　–1 Kings 19:11

DAY 61

❧

Rain!

March 1, 2014

I AWOKE THIS MORNING to falling rain—the sweetest of sounds. I live in a part of the world experiencing a devastating drought. The consequences are grave and the precipitation feels like an answer to prayer. I had almost forgotten what it was like to see water moving through the air. I stare out my window at the layers of moisture moving in concentrated patterns across the asphalt of the school playground. It's raining! What a relief. I can feel the tension dissipating as the water descends.

The local landscape has been dry and arid and now, as the storm continues to pass, the moisture makes this environment almost tropical. I can feel everything coming back to life.

These experiences remind me of the primary essentials of life: bread, water, hope, love, touch and God. We cannot survive without these elements and with them, anything becomes possible.

> *The richness of the rain made me feel safe and*
> *protected; I have always considered the rain to*
> *be healing—a blanket—the comfort of a friend.*
> *Without at least some rain in any given day,*
> *or at least a cloud or two on the horizon, I feel*
> *overwhelmed by the information of sunlight and*
> *yearn for the vital, muffling gift of falling water.*
> —Douglas Coupland,
> *Life After God*[1]

DAY 62

Cultivating Contentment

March 10, 2014

I AM NOT A MORNING PERSON.

I tend to be an individual who reluctantly gets out of bed at the last possible minute in order to meet the first deadline. For some reason, I got an early start the other day and found myself eating my breakfast in the kitchen without the need to hurry. As I sat down (*opposed to my usual practice of standing at the counter shoveling in food while multitasking*), I became aware of the sun slanting through the windows and the sound of beautiful piano music in the air. And without any effort whatsoever, I experienced a great spirit of contentment flooding my entire being. The most extraordinary sensation of well-being.

Webster's defines "contented" as *manifesting satisfaction with one's possessions, status or situation.* I wonder if it is possible to cultivate contentment. To redirect the mind away from coveting, planning, anticipating, expecting, and brooding into a more appreciative state of mind. Contentment is an unfamiliar dialect for me and I suspect, like all new languages, I will have to study its various grammatical structures in order to speak it freely. I imagine fluency with contentment begins with savoring the moment—not just the sweetness of a leisurely morning but the traffic moment, the repeating instructions moment, the arguing moment, the moment of hunger and the moment of tears.

If that sensation of satisfaction can be captured and repeated, I think I may become a contentment addict.

> *The greater part of our happiness or misery*
> *depends upon our dispositions and not upon our*
> *circumstances.*
> –Martha Washington

> *Good friends, good books and a sleepy conscience:*
> *this is the ideal life.*
> –Mark Twain

Day 63

Arresting the Thunderbolt

March 17, 2014

THERE IS A QUOTE in Rilke's *Letters to a Young Poet* in which he explains that words are inadequate instruments in attempting to describe events and experiences. Although I love words, I agree with Rilke in the impossibility of using language to define love, forgiveness or passion. However, every once in a while, a great mind is able to harness an interpretation of a moment or an experience that dazzles the reader.

The other day at morning mass, the Deacon at my parish quoted Saint John Chrysostom (*a fourth-century preacher and Bishop of Constantinople*) on the meaning and dynamics of prayer. Here is the quote—you might want to sit down for this is as good as it gets!

Prayer is an all-efficient panoply, a treasure undiminished, a mine never exhausted, a sky unobstructed by clouds, a heaven unruffled by storm. It is the root, the fountain and the mother of a thousand blessings. It exceeds a monarch's power . . . I speak not of the prayer which is cold and feeble and devoid of zeal. I speak of that which proceeds from a mind outstretched, the child of a contrite spirit, the offspring of a soul converted— this is the prayer which mounts to heaven . . . The power of prayer has subdued the strength of fire, bridled the rage of lions, silenced anarchy, extinguished wars, appeased the elements, expelled demons, burst the chains of death, enlarged the gates of heaven, relieved diseases, averted frauds, rescued cities from destruction, stayed the sun in its course and arrested the progress of the thunderbolt. In sum, prayer has power to destroy whatever is at enmity with the good.

DAY 64

Shattered

March 23, 2014

IN THE APARTMENT WHERE I LIVE above the church, there is a room I have converted into a home office. Late in the day, the sun shines in directly, inflating the area with a searing light. The other afternoon, I walked in to find that a framed print had fallen off the wall and splintered glass all over the floor. With the sun gleaming into the space it was strangely beautiful—like looking at a frozen surface in the sun. The picture must have toppled from a wall shelf, smashed into the corner of my desk and then flipped onto the floor. As I began to carefully collect the shards of glass, I found the actual print underneath the glimmering rubble—the fall had scratched the surface and marred it irreparably.

Normally my custom would be to discard something broken and unsightly. However, I cannot seem to part with the print. It cannot be replaced and it is precious to me for a multitude of reasons. For someone who has a reverence for the perfection of beauty, I find myself conflicted about how to proceed. And I have been reflecting on the preservation of those characteristics and experiences that are irregular and damaged; how we train ourselves to bury unpleasant memories, edit unattractive history and discard that which is unappealing or unpleasant. In growing older, I am discovering an interest in the transparency of the wound. I am surprisingly willing to look directly into those imperfect elements of my life and discover that same honesty refreshingly attractive in others.

I suppose I am considering having the scratched print reframed and rehung and along with it, the jagged pieces of my past and present. After all, there is a kind of beauty even when something is shattered—like pieces of ice shining in the sun.

> We are all wonderful, beautiful wrecks. That's what connects us—that we're all broken, all beautifully imperfect.
> –Emilio Estevez

> Imperfection is beauty, madness is genius and it's better to be absolutely ridiculous than absolutely boring.
> –Marilyn Monroe

DAY 65

Kiosk

March 27, 2014

THE PLACE WHERE I LIVE has a vibrant downtown. Don't you miss going downtown? Street corners and storefronts, window displays and the bustle of people coming and going in the sunshine. It's clean and bright in my downtown; everywhere you look there are students from the university, tourists, couples, and impossibly young-looking people pushing strollers with infants.

After a lunch meeting with a friend, I pulled my car in the direction of the kiosk to pay my parking fee and was confronted by an elderly, cranky-looking gentleman taking my ticket and eventually my money. He spoke with an exaggerated, comical foreign accent and as we engaged in the usual clerk-patron banter, he burst out laughing and began speaking in a predictable voice. As he inserted my parking ticket and took my cash *(an unspeakably tedious task he must repeat endlessly throughout his shift)* he explained that he was happy to be working in such a beautiful place *(a parking garage!)* and practicing speaking with a foreign accent and enjoying another beautiful day in paradise! As I drove out into the street, I was struck by his humor and goodwill. How easy it is to allow self-pity and weariness to submerge our demeanor and consequently poison the atmosphere around us. I find such people noble in their desire to extend cheer even in a busy and perfunctory setting.

Never underestimate the power of a smile, a little humor, and a kind word. These small gestures have the ability to change molecules and shift energy.

> *May the forces of evil become confused on the way*
> *to your house.*
> —George Carlin

Day 66

Kennedy

April 3, 2014

WHEN I WAS A YOUNG BOY, I could not envision a time when our nation was at war with itself. However, in the current atmosphere of political animosity, it is becoming more apparent how the desire to win trumps the common good. Consequently, I found myself moved to tears when I read this excerpt from President Kennedy's 1963 speech at American University. I am excited by anything that inspires a spirit of collaboration between nations, within family systems, and inside the human heart.

> So let us not be blind to our differences—but let
> us also direct attention to our common interests
> and to the means by which those differences
> can be resolved. And if we cannot end now our

differences, at least we can help make the world safe for diversity. For, in the final analysis, our most basic common link is that we all inhabit this small planet. We all breathe the same air, we all cherish our children's futures. And we are all mortal.

–President John F. Kennedy,
American University 1963

DAY 67

Ghost

April 8, 2014

> *Behold I tell you a mystery.*
> *Not all of us shall fall asleep,*
> *but all of us are to be changed—in an instant,*
> *in the twinkling of an eye,*
> *at the sound of the last trumpet.*
> *The trumpet will sound and the dead will be raised*
> *incorruptible, and we shall be changed.*
>
> *–Paul to the Corinthians*

FOR MOST OF MY LIFE, I did not directly experience death. All the major players in my story lived on. My grandmother died when I was in my thirties. A few years later my uncle died, then my Aunt, and about four years ago my godmother. Last year my father died and memories of him keep surfacing like depth charges. I do not necessarily feel my father's presence around me but scenes and moments from our life together replay in my mind. Unexpectedly, I will remember an expression, a tone of voice—like a scrapbook with random out-of-sequence photographs, I inexplicably envision fragments of the past.

I wonder if this is how one is haunted—not by the nocturnal rattling of chains but the popping up of clips of the past while driving the car, eating a meal or reading email. What if the crucial relationships of our lives become like scenes from a film to be replayed over and over until our words, gestures and behavior become a part of someone else's haunting?

For thirty years I have been analyzing life, death and resurrection, but there is a great divide between the academic consideration and the lived experience. How does this all work I wonder? And perhaps more profoundly . . . what will happen next?

> *There's always someone haunting someone—*
> *haunting someone.*
> *And you know who I am*
> *though I never leave my name or number.*
> *I'm locked inside of you so it doesn't matter.*
> *There's always someone haunting someone—*
> *haunting someone.*
> *And I can't sleep easy*
> *'cause I'm afraid of dreaming and then*
> *there's the memory of the dream.*
> *There's always someone haunting someone . . .*
> *Haunting someone . . .*
> *Haunting someone . . .*
>   –Carly Simon

DAY 68

Movies, Angels, and Truth

April 27, 2014

I CAN HONESTLY SAY THAT MOVIES have changed my life. Sitting in a darkened room and having a story told with actors, musical scoring, and masterful editing has educated, inspired and assisted me in processing my opinions and feelings. Having said all that, I hardly ever go to the movies anymore. I was reading a magazine yesterday highlighting all the upcoming summer films and found them all to be action heroes and animated blockbusters. Neither genre motivates me to leave the comfort of my easy chair. When I read current film reviews, I almost never feel enthusiastic about attending, and even if I do, by the time my schedule permits, the film has left the local theatre. I do watch television and find that programming to be exciting and enlightening regarding the current mood of the culture. But television series drag story-lines over months and months to sustain interest. There is something satisfying about sitting down and being told an entire story in one sitting.

Last night, I watched a movie with my mother that was completely engrossing. It was made in 1998 with Meg Ryan and Nicolas Cage entitled *City of Angels*. The film presents this idea that there are unseen angels roaming around us wearing long black duster coats and periodically assisting us in dangerous moments. Meg Ryan is a physician who is at the beginning of an existential crisis when she crosses some cosmic barrier and sees an actual angel played by Nicholas Cage. He falls in love with her and their romance is electric and mystical. The screen is filled with their eyes and faces, and the ideas presented in the film are layered and weighty. Moment after moment is wonderful, but there is one line that keeps echoing through me regarding faith. The angel and the physician are having a preliminary conversation about God and the doctor states that she does not believe, and the angel replies, "*some things are true, whether we believe them or not.*"

In a way, this feels like the message of Jesus; his content was unbelievable to the people of his time and ultimately dismissed and discarded. How often do we miss the truth and opportunity of the moment because it is inconvenient or difficult to understand? I often warn my parishioners about listening only to those whose point of view rests easily within our own convictions and prejudice. As we judge, as we select, as we categorize, are we missing the possibility of the authentic sacred in our lives simply because we don't choose to accept that which is unfamiliar? Is not one of the most wondrous facets of our God, the infinite possibilities offered in every fragment of our lives? Up to now, I have been clinging to my opinions as the foundation I function upon. Now I feel the Spirit moving me to let go of so many of my comfortably restrictive points of view and dwell in the unknown and even undesired. For truth and wisdom may sometimes exist beyond what I already know.

For some things are true whether I believe them or not.

DAY 69

Inspirational Quote

May 1, 2014

*If I were called upon to state in a few words
the essence of everything I was trying to say
both as a novelist and as a preacher, it would be
something like this: Listen to your life. See it for
the fathomless mystery that it is. In the boredom
and pain of it, no less than in the excitement and
gladness: touch, taste, smell your way to the holy
and hidden heart of it, because in the last analysis,
all moments are key moments, and life itself is
grace.*

–Frederick Buechner

Day 70

Water

May 9, 2014

The sea is emotion incarnate.
It loves, hates and weeps.
It defies all attempts to capture it with words
and rejects all shackles.
No matter what you say about it,
there is always that which you can't.
                    –Christopher Paolini, Eragon

I HAVE BEEN ATTENDING A CONFERENCE at a resort situated above the sea. There is a small winding path from the hotel undulating along the cliffs. The path rises and falls like the ocean curling and crashing below. Each day I walk that short path, or perhaps it walks me. It feels like strolling along the unfinished beams of a skyscraper—precarious—as if balancing on the edge of a great precipice.

I moved to this part of the world so that I would always be near the sea, but the ocean makes me melancholy. It is vast and grey. Even when the sun is burnishing the surface into silver—it is cold and fearsome. I love it and am endlessly fascinated; however, it will always be an inequitable relationship—like a mysterious woman loved from a distance and never to be possessed.

Day 71

Missionary Travel

May 17, 2014

THE GLAMOUR OF TRAVEL may be forever gone. Comfortable and enhancing journeys from one place to another are rare and prohibitively expensive. We are now crammed into the smallest of spaces with the bare minimum of options. Recently, while squeezing myself into a penitential-sized seat on the tiniest passenger aircraft in all Christendom, I was scolded by a fellow passenger for pausing to extract a book from my pack before placing the bag in the overhead compartment. An action that took me precisely fifteen seconds was apparently enough to aggravate this stranger into verbal antagonism. I suppose I should let it go in light of the fact that travelers these days are stressed and on edge. Security lines, automated bag checks, tart travel personnel who spend their days answering the same tedious questions—all create an environment of tension and frustration exacerbated by endless delays before ascending into the sky within the confines of a floating prison.

Little courtesies surprisingly stand out in this hostile travel world. Allowing someone ahead of you in line, offering a smile to the gate checker, returning a greeting with eye contact are shafts of sunlight on a dark and wretched day. It feels a bit like being a missionary descending into a dangerous and unpredictable environment offering hope and courage where there is fear and despair. Sometimes when I feel overwhelmed about my work and the seemingly infinite responsibilities of ministry, I remind myself my most important task is to offer kindness in whatever moment I find myself. In the sky or a traffic jam, in the market or in a mad rush—stop—breathe—practice patience . . . and miraculously the sun comes out.

Day 72

Missing a Step

May 21, 2014

I AM TRAVELING. And the other day I was dragging my suitcase across a concrete expanse and missed a step. Is there a more sickening sensation? We rushed forward confident in the ground beneath our feet only to plunge into empty space. I wrenched my knee when I crashed downward and there has been an insistent ping of pain ever since.

It reminds me of a guilty conscience sending out little signals of distress every time we remember past misbehaviors. You know what I'm talking about: the past! Those times we were cruel, indifferent or self-involved. Those missed opportunities to be generous, gracious, self-effacing surrendered instead to something less exalted. That awful ringing memory in your mind when you're tired or lonely or drunk.

Are those nightmares ever banished or do we carry them with us to the grave? Do we rewind and find the wronged party, or do we zip forward? And, more to the point, is it ever possible to advance without going backward? Is it realistic to assume that one can live life with every step placed perfectly in front of the other? Are not the most profound life lessons learned by falling and stumbling? Maybe the ache we feel on those sleepless nights is a messenger of humility reminding us how easy it is to cause suffering. Perhaps the throb can be an invitation to be mindful of the future sinkholes of greed and selfishness waiting . . . just waiting for that moment of arrogance when we step right into the trap.

> *There will be more joy in heaven over one sinner*
> *who repents than over ninety-nine righteous*
> *people who have no need of repentance.*
> –John

DAY 73

∞

Laughing at the Airport

May 28, 2014

IN THE SMALL SOUTHERN TOWN where my mother grew up, she and her sister, hungry for amusement would park on the downtown main street and people watch. I confess that I, too, find this an extremely pleasurable activity. And there is no better hunting ground for prime viewing of the human family than the airport. When traveling you see it all—the families attempting to journey with small children and their mountain of supplies, the crisp business people in their suits and teenagers who look like they just rolled out of bed and forgot to change from their pajamas. Because the public is completely absorbed in their mobile devices, it is possible to stare baldly at strangers with no fear of repercussion. I could watch for hours!

If an anthropologist questioned my perceptions based

upon my viewing, I would report an overall grim mood. Would it surprise you to know that no one is laughing at the airport? Some of these people must be taking a holiday—surely not everyone is about to defend their thesis or attend a funeral. Many of them would *appear* to be dressed for fun. Is it the stressful atmosphere of travel that makes everyone so somber or does this reflect a greater, heavier spirit pervading our culture? I cannot help but wonder: have we always been such serious people or are we becoming that way? Certainly, we have no scriptural basis of Jesus doubled over with laughter. Sadly, no gospel has the Son of God telling a joke or guffawing at the divine comedy. Nevertheless, his consistent message of forgiveness, acceptance, freedom and infinite possibilities are the foundation for joy. We surely know how to work, complain, holler, beg, desire, avoid, compensate and doubt, but do we know how to incorporate joy into the mix of our everyday human emotion?

When is the last time you had trouble breathing due to the intensity of your laughter or wiped tears from your eyes because you were filled with the buoyancy of mirth? Is not the searching for and finding of joy in each day the reason we slog on? If you are having trouble locating joy within yourself begin with gratitude. Thanksgiving is the portal to joy. And joy is the entryway to heaven!

> The glory of God is revealed in the human person
> fully alive . . .
> —Saint Irenaeus

Day 74

Free-fall . . .

June 17, 2014

I HAVE FLIGHT ANXIETY.

What's that? Priests are not supposed to have anxiety? Well, guess what? We do. Or to be more specific—this one does. I'm fine with the takeoff . . . well actually, I don't like anything about the experience. I do not like the security lines, I dislike being shoved into a miniature seat that makes me feel like I am sitting on the lap of a stranger. I am uncomfortable with surly flight attendants who treat me as if I am being sent to the principal's office. I don't like not being able to stretch or move about on a five-hour flight and I am deeply suspicious of the cleanliness of the space I am occupying. And I shall not attempt to describe the experience of a man six foot three inches tall squeezing into what passes for a restroom. However, all of this is manageable compared to the sensation of the plane in turbulence.

I do not wish to be grounded. I don't drink and cannot imagine a medication that would calm me during the flight and return me to normalcy immediately upon landing. So this brings me to the core of my problem: I hate turbulence. I know! I KNOW! I understand how the plane works and the pitching of the airliner in mid-air is merely a "bump in the road." I have been educated in the knowledge that I am safe and that statistics demonstrate that I am in greater danger crossing the street than zipping across the heavens......but once that shuddering and dropping begins—I feel panic. Not distress. Not discomfort. **PANIC!**

So two weeks ago on a flight from Atlanta to Los Angeles we entered into some prolonged bumpy weather. I practiced my breathing. I refreshed my meditation. I began to pray the Rosary. But while all these tools brought a modicum of comfort, I knew I was inexorably slipping into a major anxiety attack. At some point in the middle of the pitching and praying it occurred to me that this feeling must be akin to being told one has inoperable cancer. This could be the exact way a parent feels when told their child is in danger. Free-falling. It's terrifying to plunge into an uncontrollable situation. However, are we ever truly in authority of any circumstance? Is the mirage of control so seductive that we believe that it exists? After all, it only takes a bleak diagnosis, a negative performance review or extended turbulence to face the shattering realization that control is an illusion.

Perhaps we are free falling all the time with only brief intervals of groundedness. I began to wonder: what if life is actually all about the free-fall and how we handle it? If life is intended to be a cosmic classroom for learning lessons and the most profound teaching comes from adversity, is it conceivable that we are meant to learn stability through repeated episodes of turbulence and the episodes of calm are merely re-fueling stations where we catch our breath before the next drop? Like a student of martial arts who learns to fall safely after being tossed into the air, what if the meaning of life is not comfort but an on-going exercise in stabilization in the midst of turmoil? What if, after a lifetime of turbulence, we finally learn there is nothing to be afraid of?

DAY 75

Summer Bliss

July 17, 2014

Summer Afternoon—summer afternoon, to me those have always been the two most beautiful words in the English language.
    –Henry James

LOVE THIS TIME OF YEAR. Warmth, sunshine and the slow transition from light into darkness at the end of the day. I am aware that summertime in different parts of the country is hot and humid with unpleasant heat and dangerous storms. Last year I was in New York City in July and no matter what preparations I would take, after walking two blocks from my hotel, I would be crumpled and deflated. I have lived in parts of California with endless foggy days—horrible summers where it was necessary to put on a jacket before going outside and resisting the urge to activate the electric heat when indoors . . . *in August!* However, the place I now inhabit is enjoying an idyllic summer. We have been waking up to foggy mornings cooling the remainder of the day and mid-morning sunshine breaking through the mist revealing bright days designed for wearing shorts and sandals.

One afternoon last week I sat on the steps where I live reading a novel and enjoying the sun on my legs. It was one of those perfect moments when one is sitting outdoors and neither too hot nor too cold. I suppose this time of year reminds me of my childhood summers when my only responsibility was mowing the lawn, emptying the garbage or setting the table for supper. And although now my life continues to be filled with the usual tasks of preaching, planning, anointing and administrating there is still that summertime fragrance of ease and languor. At times like this, I hope the Kingdom of Heaven is one long eternal summer afternoon.

DAY 76

⚜

In Praise of the
Everyday Hero

July 30, 2014

*Heroes are ordinary people who make themselves
extraordinary.*
            –Gerard Way

RECENTLY I HAD MY TEETH CLEANED. In spite of my familiarity with
this procedure, it never fails to surprise me how unnerving it is
to have so many objects simultaneously inserted into my mouth.
Suction devices compete with misting water and fingers holding
instruments scraping and polishing the teeth. All these elements
are being manipulated by the hygienist in a manner of complete
nonchalance. While trapped in her lair, it occurred to me how
awkward it must be for her to be hunched over a patient while
attempting to clean a complicated and irregular environment.

Imagine being her. Each day facing a long series of clients with varied temperaments and responses to what is an invasive and uncomfortable circumstance. And yet, every six months I find her to be unfailingly gracious and encouraging. I have never known her to complain about neck or shoulder pain. Never does she express self-pity at the dreariness of her daily task but instead makes an effort to present to the world a pleasant and get-the-job-done attitude.

I have great appreciation for those who approach their daily task with good will and humor. There is a heroism I associate with the person who chooses to live and work with hope and courage. The truth is that we all face daily tasks full of tedium. Even James Bond 007 must dread another lengthy expedition to a foreign port, yet another arch-enemy to be outwitted, and one more exhausting seduction to be orchestrated!

Every life is full of back pain and money problems. Each human person is struggling to overcome the past and brace for the future. The cashier at the grocery store who extends a smile and a greeting to literally hundreds of daily customers is a hero to me. So here's to all the people who perform repetitive acts of service with style and zeal. They make the daily hurdle a little more manageable.

> *Everybody is special. Everybody. Everybody is a*
> *hero, a lover, a fool, a villain. Everybody has their*
> *story to tell.*
> −Alan Moore

DAY 77

Learn to Be Lonely

August 26, 2014

Child of the wilderness
Born into emptiness
Learn to be lonely
Learn to find your way in the darkness

Who will be there for you
Comfort and care for you
Learn to be lonely
Learn to be your one companion

Never dreamed out in the world
there are arms to hold you
You've always known your heart was on its own

So laugh in your loneliness
Child of the wilderness
Learn to be lonely
Learn how to love life that is lived alone

Learn to be lonely
Life can be lived, life can be loved alone. [1]

> –Andrew Lloyd Webber, Richard Henry
> Zachary Stilgoe, Charles Elliott Hart,
> "Learn to be Lonely Song" *Phantom of
> the Opera*

I HAVE BEEN THINKING ABOUT LONELINESS LATELY. And not just my own but the aloneness that is experienced by all people in every form of living. The isolation of the divorced, widowed, the unpopular, the maimed, the elderly, those in the hospital, and the marginalized. I have been considering the conditioning that infiltrates our upbringing; the terror of keeping one's own company. How often do we make undesirable social choices in order to avoid the tragic possibility of being lonely?

Obviously, loneliness affects all of us regardless of the size of our family or the success of our primary relationships, and yet for most of us, the thought of being unaccompanied is akin to being trapped in a nightmare. Elizabeth Gilbert in her famous book *Eat, Pray, Love* writes, "When I get lonely these days, I think: so BE lonely Liz. Learn your way around loneliness. Make a map of it. Sit with it, for once in your life. Welcome to the human experience. But never again use another person's body or emotions as a scratching post for your own unfulfilled yearnings."

I cannot help but wonder if it is possible to befriend loneliness—not to merely fill it with entertainments and distractions but as Gilbert suggests: "*sit with it.*" To examine the size and atmosphere of being alone and thereby tame and minimize the dread accompanying that state of being. Ultimately, I suppose loneliness is a complex package, wrapped and encircled with the issues of self-esteem, God, love, desirability, perspective and time. Nevertheless, with whatever time I have I left, I want to extinguish as much energy devoted to fear as possible. Wouldn't it be wonderful to be at the end of one's life and be afraid of nothing?

All great and precious things are lonely.
   –John Steinbeck, *East of Eden*

The most terrible poverty is loneliness and the feeling of being unloved.
   –Mother Theresa

Day 78

Euphoria in the Minefields

September 19, 2014

EVERY HUMAN PERSON CAN DESCRIBE in searing detail the most awkward time in their life. For me, it was the middle school and early high school timeframe that makes me wince. I suddenly, supernaturally shot up in height beyond my peers and the vertical growth brought on a humiliating lack of coordination. I was forever dropping the baseball, extricating myself from the tangle of my own legs and slamming my shoulder into door-frames. It was at this supreme moment of awkwardness my skin broke out and having spent my early childhood in the school uniform of Catholic schools, found myself bewildered about what to wear to a public high school. My sartorial confusion resulted in trousers invariably too short at the ankles and too wide around the waist. I could go on but you get the picture.

In my sophomore year, I was invited to join the staff of the school yearbook edited by a demigod. HE was of a normal height and the highest-ranking member of the honor roll. He was handsome, could sing, wrote beautifully, was a superb athlete, an easy conversationalist with boys and girls—in short: your basic nightmare! My admiration made it impossible to actually envy or resent such a staggering specimen, but he did provide me with an image of aspiration. I could never compete but I could attempt to imitate. We became superficial friends and attended the same university.

At the conclusion of the second year of undergraduate studies, he inexplicably took his own life.

It's difficult to describe the darkness that swallowed me at that time. Although we were never close friends, I admired him and wanted to be like him. It was unimaginable that such a gifted and superior individual would think so little of his enormous persona that he could abandon all future possibilities and the fulfillment of such obvious advantages. At this time in my life, I was a runner and some weeks after his death, I found myself on the track when the cloud of my depression unexpectedly dissipated. I felt this surge of the life force within me—sad about the ending of my mentor's life but buoyant with the opportunities and adventures that awaited me in living. Even then I knew there would be black days, tears and setbacks, but the desire to keep moving forward and the quest for the unfolding of my story gave me a great spirit of anticipation.

Recently I received some rather worrisome news about my health. At this stage, there is no cause for alarm but the original diagnosis was a jolt, and I felt a paralyzing sense of fear and a new and unwelcome awareness of my own mortality. Initially, after my medical consultation, I became mired in an ominous atmosphere of dread and then again, the unexpected lifting of my spirit to a place of gratitude and hope. I do not know from where that life preserver was tossed, I only know how grateful I am to be alive today. To walk by the sea, to eat pasta, to lift my voice in sung prayer to God, to listen to my mother's voice, to engage my body in motion (*these days on an elliptical machine*) the crackling sound of the spine in the opening of a new book or the exquisite feeling of laughter rising up from my belly—these are the moments I live for. I wish I could explain this strange phenomenon but I know not how. I only know that I live in a beautiful place, have work that brings me great purpose and friends who enrich my life, and these wonders are enough to sustain me in my journey through the minefield.

DAY 79

C3

The End of the Love Affair

October 10, 2014

I THINK THE LOVE AFFAIR BEGAN when I was just a child.

There was some undefinable pleasure in making my bed, shelving my toys, books and games, and hanging my clothes in just the right spot. Something so seductive, even for a child, in creating order. However, like an alcoholic who gets that first taste of liquor, this particular pleasure had an appetite and gradually, almost imperceptibly, I found myself attempting to control every aspect of my life. In some ways, it is a fantastic way to live—the belief that everything is in its exact place. There is a deep satisfaction in being able to put your hand on exactly the document, book, quote, feeling and personality one needs. The knowledge that your life is neat and tidy like a well-made bed enables you to sleep soundly at night.

And then, quite rudely, you are made aware that control is a glorious illusion.

The dissipation of control happens in small ways throughout one's life: a disappointing grade in one's academic effort, an argument that escalates into a permanent estrangement, a rejection, a diagnosis and ultimately the dark, worrisome day when a total stranger wheels you into an operating room so another stranger can open your body with a knife. Those are the moments when one realizes the depth and breadth of powerlessness.

I've always believed that control was power but maybe I was wrong—perhaps the real strength is to be found in recognizing our power-*lessness*. For all the attempted control in the world can't keep the cancer cells from multiplying, the forest fires from burning and the destructive encroachment of identity theft. What if once we stop grasping it becomes possible to trust, and in trusting . . . find peace? After all, we enter this world in a powerless state and if lucky enough to live a long life, end powerlessly. What if the real quest is to acknowledge our vulnerability and even embrace our dependence? What if the great revelation of our lives is that control is nothing more than a fantasy . . . a glorious illusion?

> *The Lord is my shepherd;*
> *I shall not want*
> *In verdant pastures he gives me repose;*
> *beside restful waters he leads me;*
> *he refreshes my soul.*
> *He guides me in right paths for*
> *his name's sake.*

Even though I walk in the dark
valley I fear no evil
for you are at my side
with your rod and your staff
that give me courage.
        –Psalm 23

Day 80

This Is Who You Really Are

October 23, 2014

L AST WEEK I WENT TO SAN FRANCISCO with my niece attending a book signing and live interview with an author of contemporary essays. At one point in the interview, the writer was asked about the major influences in her life. All the way home I began to ask myself the same question: who and what are the significant events and personalities who have directed the trajectory of my life? Have you ever asked yourself that question? What circumstances have caused you to turn, move, accept and evolve? I suspect that love is the greatest of motivators. Nature, ambition, greed, desire, lust, spirituality and hope all contain compelling directional forces.

Once when I was in college, I was captivated by a movie unfolding in the undersea world of scuba diving. So compelling was that story, I enrolled in a class, went to Mexico, and became certified as a diver. Certainly, the planet is full of people who abandon everything familiar and explore parts unknown to climb a mountain, cure the sick and seek the meaning of life. How intriguing to consider at any moment we could read a book, have a conversation, watch a segment on the news and be propelled into another world. Sometimes, I suspect, these revelations are like depth charges that gestate for years and ultimately reveal themselves in moments of transition.

How extraordinary to consider that we are the summation of an infinite array of influences—parents, teachers, spiritual leaders, friends, literature, art, travel, academia, dreams, conversations, home, and passion are the individual puzzle pieces of the person we are today. If we are what we eat, then are we not also shaped and styled by the dynamic circumstances and personalities of our lives? I cannot help but wonder if we made a list of all the major influences on our journey and study that list, would we not finally see who we really are?

> *Self-rejection is the greatest enemy of the spiritual life because it contradicts the sacred voice that calls us "Beloved," Being the "Beloved" is the core truth of our existence.*
> –Henri J.M. Nouwen

> *We know what we are, but not what we may be.*
> –William Shakespeare

Day 81

CB

Courtesy in the Jungle

November 12, 2014

A YEAR AGO, I went to New York City with my niece where we stayed at the top of a shabby but venerable hotel. Each day we left our rooms and entered the elevator as its sole occupants. As the transport descended to the urban floor, it would become populated with more and more people. Every New York City day I would greet those entering the elevator. I would smile and offer a "good morning!"

I suppose my innocent looking companion and my neat demeanor squashed their suspicions, but my niece was horrified. She would stare straight ahead and later question why it was necessary to address total strangers who would never be seen or heard from again! I'm not sure if I have the answer to her question; I only know that it brings me pleasure to offer courtesy when I enter public spaces.

My parents grew up in a southern region of the United States, and when visiting that part of the country, I always notice the gracious way people interact. It appears to be such a civilized way of living, to respectfully acknowledge the presence of another person. These small acts of courtesy smooth away the rough edges of everyday life. When wrestling with parcels, are you not grateful when a stranger opens a door for you to pass through? Once when waiting at a luggage carousel in a small southern airport, a stranger lifted my heavy bag off the conveyor and handed it over the mountains of holiday suitcases . . . with a smile . . . and actually spoke the words, *Merry Christmas!* Moments like that are a breath of fresh air in the madding world of holiday travel.

The unvarnished fact is that our world is becoming harsher and full of stress. I am frequently mortified by the expressions of indifference and entitlement I witness in the marketplace. To offer kindness or courtesy in mundane settings is an expression of nobility. I cannot promise you that your efforts will be rewarded or even acknowledged, but there is a refreshing lift that comes from transcending one's personal preoccupations and extending goodwill to a stranger. Sometimes what you get in return is an on-rushing of pure gratitude. And perhaps . . . just perhaps . . . your gestures, your efforts, commingle with mine, to make our world a little bit more peaceful, more hopeful, more holy.

Here, on the pulse of this new day
You may have the grace to look up and out
And into your sister's eyes, and into
Your brother's face, your country
And say simply
Very simply
With hope—
Good morning.

        –Maya Angelou

Day 82

Passwords, Codes, and Secrets

December 10, 2014

I N LAST SUNDAY'S *NEW YORK TIMES*, Ian Urbina wrote a remarkable (*and lengthy*) article about the designing of our passwords.[1] He details how passwords are the new keys opening the doors of our various internet worlds.

> *Several years ago, I began asking my friends and family to tell me their passwords. I had come to believe that these tiny personalized codes get a bum rap. Yes, I understand why passwords are universally despised: the strains they put on our memory, the endless demand to update them, their annoyance. In our authorship of them, in the fact that we construct them so that we (and*

*only we) will remember them, they take on secret
lives. Many of our passwords are suffused with
pathos, mischief, sometimes even poetry. Often
they have rich backstories. A motivational mantra,
a swipe at the boss, a hidden shrine to a lost love,
an inside joke with ourselves, a defining emotional
scar—these keepsake passwords, as I came to
call them, are like tchotchkes of our inner lives.
They derive from anything: scripture, horoscopes,
nicknames, lyrics, book passages. Like a tattoo on a
private part of the body, they tend to be intimate,
compact and expressive.*

I am intrigued by the idea that our lives necessitate the creation
of small coded passwords in order to operate in the technological
atmosphere. And in order to make this cipher memorable, these
passwords often reflect intimate landmarks. It is fascinating
to consider that every day we employ keywords that reflect
circumstances and memories decoded by the individual alone.
This refreshes my awareness of the profound inner lives of others.
Often I am in danger of assuming that people are exactly what
they present to the world. Am I the totality of what I present to
the world? Are you? Are we not all an amalgamation of history,
relationships, dreams, successes, failures and longings? And
don't we all present to society a mere fraction of the whole inner
person?

How easy it is to dismiss, judge, assume and move on without
recognizing that everyone has fallen in love, been rejected,
recovered from illness, and nurtures undisclosed truths. I can't

help but wonder if that information makes it a little easier to be patient with the neighbor and the stranger during this busy time of year. And if recognizing that within everyone there is that which is unknown and unrevealed, can we not extend a greater level of respect for the courage within the person next to us, who in spite of shame, anxiety or secrets has chosen to get out of bed, wash their face and walk into a new day?

> *Man is not what he thinks he is,*
> *he is what he hides.*
>> – Andre Malraux

DAY 83

☙

Windows

December 31, 2014

The eyes are the windows to the soul.

S EVERAL TIMES A WEEK, I get called to the nearby hospital to anoint someone who is gravely ill or dying. I approach this responsibility with great trepidation. You cannot anticipate what the atmosphere will be when you enter the room. Sometimes I find an elderly person alone and unconscious. At times the room is packed with family summoned to the bedside of a relative unexpectedly stricken or injured. Crying, stoicism and hysteria are all possibilities when entering the hospital room, and I consistently wonder if I possess the necessary resources to bring serenity and hope into a volatile situation.

Recently I received a call from an Emergency Room nurse,

who informed me that a young woman preparing to be married in two weeks had been struck by an automobile and was being kept on life support until I could arrive to administer the Sacrament of the Sick. She was still in the OR when I arrived, and the staff had allowed her large family into the space. The entire expanse was filled with despair. After I had concluded the prayer, the group dispersed into the hallway. As I prepared to depart and was saying goodbye, I found myself directly in front of the victim's mother. Instead of voicing the usual phrases and messages, I instinctively touched her arm and looked directly into her eyes for a moment. I may never know what she interpreted from that encounter, but I allowed my gaze to express sorrow for her loss and condolence in her unimaginable pain.

The poet Rilke once wrote that words are inadequate vessels to express deeply felt emotions, and in spite of my love of language, I'm inclined to agree. There are experiences and feelings that simply cannot be summed up verbally. Sometimes it is enough to merely look directly into the eyes of another person and allow your compassion to shine forth. Perhaps all that is required when approaching someone on their worst day is allowing them to see that you are there.

In the aftermath of this Emergency Room event, I have found myself speaking less and looking more. After all, when I am broken, wounded or lost, do I really need someone to tell me they know exactly how I feel? When grieving, does anyone need to be reminded that the deceased is in a better place? I suspect that what we all want on that black day is to have someone hold our hand, look into our eyes with an expression that lets us know that they see how bad it is, and no matter what will always love us.

> The soul, fortunately, has an interpreter
> —often an unconscious, but still a faithful
> interpreter—in the eye.
>> – Charlotte Bronte, *Jane Eyre*

DAY 84

Past Imperfect

March 1, 2015

S O, I'M READING THIS NOVEL. It's a thriller. England. Rain. A fatal accident. Or *was* it? Atmospheric. Menacing. I'm in heaven! When suddenly I realize that this is not the first novel in the series. This book is the third in a *continuing* series! *I'M IN THE MIDDLE OF THIS CHARACTER'S STORY!! No, no, no. I have to start at the beginning.* Something about the fact that this character has a past (however fictional) is ruining everything! I close the book and reserve the original at the library. Even as I surrender to what I know is a compulsive behavior, I can't help but ponder the power yesterday holds over today. How often do we allow the past to paralyze us? Why do we let our history with all its limitations and expansions affect our present and future?

Jesus is all about today. When he invites virtual strangers to come to live with him, he never questions their past or asks for a resume. He merely makes an invitation to follow, join, change and be open to the adventure of right now. I wonder if it is possible to approach each new day without being shackled by the past. What if we were to approach our daily challenges with the knowledge that our past, however flawed, provides us with a reservoir of knowledge, wisdom and experience that will assist us in our ongoing development?

I suppose the past can either be a prison or a resource center. I suspect that all of us need to release the jeering and the medals, the touchdowns and the fall downs. The triumphs and the disappointments belong in the scrapbook, not in the discernment of what I can or cannot do today. Recently I have been made aware that today is all we have . . . it's all we've ever had.

> *Yesterday is gone. Tomorrow has not yet come.*
> *We have only today. Let us begin.*
>   – Mother Teresa

> *We are products of our past, but we don't have to*
> *be prisoners of it.*
>   – Rick Warren

Day 85

Images

May 26, 2015

ONCE UPON A TIME, I was friendly with a large extended family inhabiting the town where I served as a priest. This clan possessed a ranch house in the country where they gathered annually to swim, barbecue, nap and read. On one occasion many years ago, I spent a few days in their company and witnessed a moment that clings to me. One of the children got out of the pool while his mother squatted down and enfolded him in a large fluffy beach towel. Drying him in the sunshine, she asked what he would like to eat for lunch. It was such a non-moment, but there was a quality of undivided attentiveness that tugged at me with longing.

Generally, I don't remember having such moments with my parents. It seems to me they were forever wanting us out from underfoot. They were delighted for me to be sequestered in my childhood bedroom reading novels. Banished when their adult friends came visiting and generally unimpressed with my witty teenage observations about life. For the longest time after that pool moment, I bathed in a warm bath of self-pity, immersing myself in the belief that I had been ignored and unappreciated as a child. That observation was a key that unlocked a room of discontent and resentment.

And then, unexpectedly, another observation occurred that shifted that view. I was watching an old home movie with early scenes from my parents' marriage and sequences featuring my brother and myself as little children. Like a Time Machine, the film transported me back to an instance where my mother was feeding my baby brother. He was encased in an old-fashioned "high chair" (*do those still exist?*), and my mother is sitting across from him, carefully spooning soft food into his mouth with complete absorption. He is clearly content and well cared for, and she is weary, young and beautiful. And just like that, a million images reentered my memory: my parents sitting on baseball field bleachers, even when I was *unplayed*. Recitals, plays, awards ceremonies—a waterfall of events they endured while I performed or commenced. There they were, making sure I had clothes, shoes that fit, piano lessons and an education. With one image, another door was opened—a vantage point where I could see clearly their endless sacrifices, their pride in their children, reservoirs of love and dreams for our happiness.

Perhaps life really is what we look at—what we choose to remember. I suspect we often get stuck gazing at one particular frame: the image where we are unappreciated, unnoticed or thwarted. Gazing too long at such an image can enable us to lose our perspective.

If we want to be a hopeful, optimistic people, it's time to start paying attention to the abundance, not the deficit. What if we curated a splay of positive mental images we scan regularly, like the photos on our phone? Whenever we feel lost, defeated or shut down we sort through those great moments of triumph, wonder or tenderness and just like that . . . our spirit begins to rise.

> *You don't make a photograph just with a camera.*
> *You bring to the act of photography all the*
> *pictures you have seen, the books you have read,*
> *the music you have heard, the people you have*
> *loved.*
>
> – Ansel Adams

Epilogue

Each day is a brand-new life.
–Frank Wildhorn

THERE HAVE BEEN NOVELS WRITTEN that take place within one single day of the character's life. The suggestion is that everything we need to know about a person is to be found within the context of a day. From the moment we rise until we rest, there are a myriad of experiences that reveal who we really are. When you keep a journal and return to it in the future, it is extraordinary how the questions we ask ourselves, the people we encounter and our reactions on any given day can surprise and enlighten us. After living for eighteen years in the blur of a congested atmosphere, I came to a smaller, more rural place to answer some questions about my life and ministry. Knowing that I would have more time for reflection, I kept this journal to assist in achieving clarity and understanding.

Within each day are a multitude of possibilities, and in that frame, we have the great privilege of asking questions, seeking fulfillment and acquiring knowledge. May we all find beauty, nourishment and contentment in the passing of our days. There is a remarkable journey to be found every single day.

Each day is a brand-new life . . .

Father Matt Pennington ~

References

DAY 5:
1. Friedman, Thomas L. 2013. "Bring On the Next Marathon." https://www.nytimes.com/2013/04/17/opinion/friedman-bring-on-the-next-marathon.html

DAY 12:
1. Nazarian, Vera. 2010. *The Perpetual Calendar of Inspiration,* Vermont: Norilana Books.

DAY 16:
1. Walls, Jeannette. 2013l "How Jeannette Walls Spins Good Stories Out of Bad Memories" https://www.nytimes.com/2013/05/26/magazine/how-jeannette-walls-spins-good-stories-out-of-bad-memories.html

DAY 17:
1. Luhrmann, Tanya. 2013 "Why Belief is the Leaset Part of Faith." https://www.nytimes.com/2013/05/30/opinion/luhrmann-belief-is-the-least-part-of-faith.html.

DAY 19:
1. Friedman, Thomas L. 2013. "How to Get a Job." https://www.nytimes.com/2013/05/29/opinion/friedman-how-to-get-a-job.html

DAY 37:
1. McBrien, Richard P. 1994 . *Encyclopedia of Catholicism.* NYC: Harper-Collins Publishers.

DAY 41:
1. Kenny, John. 2013. *Truth in Advertising.* NYC: Touchstone/Simon and Schuster.

Day 43:
1. Hosseini, Khaled. 2003. *The Kite Runner. NYC:* Penguin Group.

Day 47:
1. McBrien, Richard P. 1994 . *Encyclopedia of Catholicism.* NYC: Harper-Collins Publishers.

Day 52:
1. Brown, Tina. 2013. "Tina Brown on the Obamacare Cock-Up" https://www.thedailybeast.com/tina-brown-on-the-obamacare-cock-up

Day 57:
1. David Benioff, David. 2009. *City of Thieves* NYC: Penguin Books

Day 61:
1. Coupland, Douglas. 1994. *Life After God.* NYC: Pocket Books/ Simon & Schuster

Day 77:
1. Webber, Andrew Lloyd. 2004. "Learn to be Lonely" *Phantom of the Opera.* https://www.lyrics.com/lyric/9115393/Andrew+Lloyd+Webber

Day 82:
1. Urbina, Ian. 2014. "The Secret Life of Passwords: Reporter's Notebook." https://www.nytimes.com/times-insider/2014/12/01/the-secret-life-of-passwords-reporters-notebook/?rref=collection%2Fbyline%2Fian-urbina&action=click&contentCollection=undefined&region=stream&module=stream_

CPSIA information can be obtained
at www.ICGtesting.com
Printed in the USA
JSHW022023180422
24918JS00001B/3

9 781942 497455